Graphing Calculator Activities for Glencoe Algebra 1

Integration • Applications • Connections

Dr. Deborah A. Haver
Glenn E. Gould
Dr. Jane A. McDonald

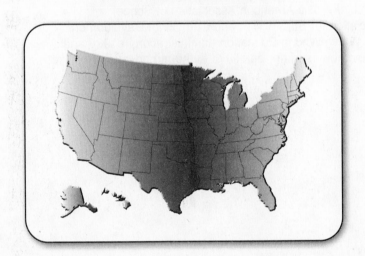

 **Glencoe McGraw-Hill**

New York, New York   Columbus, Ohio   Woodland Hills, California   Peoria, Illinois

Dr. Deborah A. Haver is an Assistant Principal at Great Bridge Middle School in Chesapeake, Virginia. She received her B.S. and M.S.Ed. from Old Dominion University in Norfolk, Virginia. She also earned an Educational Specialist in Administration and Supervision and a Doctorate in Educational Administration and Policy Studies/Executive Leadership from The George Washington University in Washington, D.C. Dr. Haver was elected among Who's Who Among American Outstanding Young Women in America in 1985. She is also active in NCTM, is president of the Virginia Council for Mathematics Supervision, and has held several offices in the Tidewater Council of Teachers of Mathematics.

Glenn E. Gould is a teacher of mathematics and an educational consultant at Liberty High School in Bealeton, Virginia. He received his B.A. and M.B.A. from the State University of New York. Mr. Gould is well versed in the use of graphing calculators and is an experienced *CASIO CFX-9850Ga PLUS* Calculator Trainer and Texas Instrument Trainer. He is also active in NCTM, Virginia Council for Mathematics Supervision, and the Tidewater Council of Teachers of Mathematics.

Dr. Jane A. McDonald is an Associate Professor of Educational Leadership at The George Washington University in Washington, D.C. Dr. McDonald received her B.A. from the University of Florida and her M.A.Ed., C.A.G.S., and Ed.D. from Virginia Polytechnic Institute and State University. She belongs to numerous professional organizations including The American Association of School Administrators and the Association for Supervision and Curriculum Development. Dr. McDonald was named to Who's Who in Education Administration in 1988 and has received many awards and honors in her pursuit of furthering advanced education.

Glencoe/McGraw-Hill

A Division of The McGraw-Hill Companies

Send all inquiries to:
Glencoe/McGraw-Hill
8787 Orion Place
Columbus, OH 43240

ISBN: 0-02-834439-1   *Glencoe Algebra 1 Graphing Calculator Activities*

2 3 4 5 6 7 8 9 10   066   03 02 01 00

Contents

Correlation to Glencoe's *Algebra 1: Integration, Applications, and Connections* iv

An Introduction to the Graphing Calculator
    Introduction to the *CASIO CFX-9850GA PLUS* Graphics Calculator 1
    Introduction to the Texas Instruments TI-83 Graphing Calculator 6

Lesson 1   *Solving Linear Inequalities in One Variable*
    Teaching Suggestions 10
    CASIO CFX-9850Ga PLUS Keystrokes 13
    TI-83 Keystrokes 15
    Student Worksheet 17

Lesson 2   *Solving Equations with the Variable on Both Sides*
    Teaching Suggestions 18
    CASIO CFX-9850Ga PLUS Keystrokes 21
    TI-83 Keystrokes 24
    Student Worksheet 27

Lesson 3   *Basic Matrix Operations:*
    Addition, Subtraction, and Scalar Multiplication
    Teaching Suggestions 28
    CASIO CFX-9850Ga PLUS Keystrokes 32
    TI-83 Keystrokes 34
    Student Worksheet 36

Lesson 4   *Recognizing Patterns:*
    Investigating Algebraic Relationships in Regular Polygons
    Teaching Suggestions 37
    Regular Polygons Master 40
    CASIO CFX-9850Ga PLUS Keystrokes 41
    TI-83 Keystrokes 48
    Student Worksheet 55

Lesson 5   *Analyzing Linear Equations*
    Teaching Suggestions 56
    CASIO CFX-9850Ga PLUS Keystrokes 57
    Casio Student Worksheet 58
    TI-83 Keystrokes 59
    TI-83 Student Worksheet 60

Lesson 6   *Solving Systems of Linear Equations*
    Teaching Suggestions 61
    CASIO CFX-9850Ga PLUS Keystrokes 63
    TI-83 Keystrokes 66
    Student Worksheet 69

Lesson 7   *Exploring Quadratic Functions*
    Teaching Suggestions 70
    CASIO CFX-9850Ga PLUS Keystrokes 76
    TI-83 Keystrokes 79
    Student Worksheets 82

Lesson 8   *M^3—Mean, Median, and Mode*
    Teaching Suggestions 84
    CASIO CFX-9850Ga PLUS Keystrokes 87
    TI-83 Keystrokes 90
    Student Worksheets 93

Overview

This booklet contains an introduction to the basic operations of the *CASIO CFX-9850Ga PLUS* and the TI-83 graphing calculators. It also contains eight graphing calculator lessons that are correlated to Glencoe's *Algebra 1: Integration, Applications, and Connections.*

Each lesson is composed of four parts:

- Teaching suggestions with hints for using each type of calculator and answers,

- Tutorial lesson featuring keystroke instructions for the *CASIO CFX-9850Ga PLUS* calculator,

- Tutorial lesson featuring keystroke instructions for the TI-83 calculator, and a

- Student Worksheet for students to practice what they have learned from the tutorial.

	Correlation to *Glencoe Algebra 1: Integration, Applications, and Connections*	
Lesson	**Title**	***Glencoe Algebra 1: Integration, Applications, and Connections***
1	Solving Linear Inequalities in One Variable	Chapter 7
2	Solving Equations with the Variable on Both Sides	Chapter 3
3	Basic Matrix Operations	Chapter 2
4	Recognizing Patterns	Chapters 1 and 5
5	Analyzing Linear Equations	Chapter 6
6	Solving Systems of Linear Equations	Chapter 8
7	Exploring Quadratic Functions	Chapter 11
8	M^3—Mean, Median, and Mode	Chapters 3 and 7

Introduction to the CASIO CFX-9850Ga PLUS Graphics Calculator

This section provides helpful hints and specific information about using the *CASIO CFX-9850Ga PLUS* calculator. If you own a *CASIO CFX-9850G* calculator, you may find that you need slightly different keystrokes than those provided in this booklet. Refer to your User's Guide for the keying sequence you need to perform the same functions.

Function keys and menus

- The `F1`, `F2`, `F3`, `F4`, `F5`, and `F6` keys are referred to as soft function keys. The `EXIT` key retraces the button path of these keys.

NOTE: The name of the function accessed by the soft function keys, the `SHIFT` key, or the `ALPHA` keys will appear in brackets after the key used to access the function.

- Always, *"When in doubt, exit out!"*
- All error messages, such as **MA ERROR**, **DIM ERROR**, and so on, can only be cleared using the `AC/ON` button.
- The `F↔D` key (changing fractional answers to decimals and vice versa) will not function if the **Image Set** is not **Off**. This feature is found in the **LINK Mode** at the **MAIN MENU**.

RUN Mode

- In the **RUN Mode**, press `AC/ON` and then the up or down arrows to recall and redisplay previous calculations—the sequence being the newest to the oldest (multi-replay function). If you leave the **RUN Mode** and then return back to the **RUN Mode**, the previous calculations will be gone.
- If a picture is superimposed over a graph or a double axis appear, check to see if the **Background** setting in the **RUN Mode** is set to **NONE**.

Set Contrast

- You can control the darkness of the image and adjust the color of the images on the screen.
- Press and select **CONT Mode** by pressing `ALPHA` `COS` [E]. You can also select it by using the arrow keys to select the **CONT** icon and press `EXE`.
- Set **Contrast: orange, blue, green** by selecting one of two choices: `F1` [INIT] changes the contrast of highlighted color to the default setting. `F2` [IN-A] changes the contrast of all colors to the default setting.

Set Viewing Window

- Select the **RUN Mode**, by pressing `MENU` 1. Pressing `SHIFT` displays **ZOOM** above `F2`, **V-WIN** above `F3`, **SKTCH** above `F4`, and `G↔T` above `F6`.

Introduction

- Press **F3** [V-WIN] to access the **View Window**. It shows the current settings for a coordinate grid. You can change each setting manually by scrolling down and entering the desired value or you can select preset windows by pressing **F1**, **F2**, or **F3**.

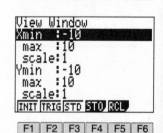

  F1 [INIT] This is the initial setting. It provides a square coordinate window. Graphs appear similarly to those graphed on grid paper. Multiples of these values will also produce the square window.

  F3 [STD] This is the standard coordinate window, often referenced as the standard viewing window or a [−10, 10] by [−10, 10] coordinate grid.

  F4 [STO] Allows you to store different window settings for future use.

  F5 [RCL] Allows you to recall your window settings.

  EXIT Returns you to **RUN Mode**.

SET UP in RUN Mode

- To access **SETUP** from the **Run Mode**, press **SHIFT** **MENU**. The default settings are shown at the right. Scroll down to see other choices.

Selecting Function Type

- You can select the type of equation or inequality you want to enter by highlighting **Func Type**, pressing **F6** [▷], and then using the soft function keys to select the type of inequality or equation you desire. Pressing **F6** again will give you other options.

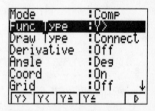

Graph the inequality y > −2.

Enter the inequality. From the **SETUP Mode**, press **F6** [▷], **F1** [Y>] **EXIT** **MENU** 5 [GRAPH] (−) 2 **EXE**. Now observe the calculator's graphing and shading capabilities by pressing **F6** [DRAW]. To delete the graph, press **EXIT**, highlight **Y1 > −2**, and press **F2** [DEL] **F1** [YES].

Introduction to the CASIO CFX-9850Ga PLUS Graphics Calculator (continued)

Graph x = 4 (a vertical line).

Press MENU 1 [RUN] SHIFT MENU [SET UP]. Highlight **Func Type** and select F4 [X=C]. Press EXIT MENU 5 [GRAPH] and enter **4**. Then press EXE. *Notice what happened on the left.* Press F6 [DRAW] EXIT . Clear the graph and equation by highlighting **X1 = 4** and pressing F2 [DEL] F1 [YES].

Selecting Display

- Return to the **SET UP** menu: MENU 1 [RUN] SHIFT MENU SET UP. Highlight **Func Type** and select F1 [Y=]. Use the arrow key to scroll down to **Display**.

  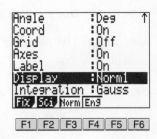

  Norm 1 displays nonrepeating rational numbers to two decimal places; at three-decimal places, it converts the result to scientific notation.

  Norm 2 displays nonrepeating rational numbers to nine decimal places; at ten decimal places, it converts to scientific notation.

- Pressing F3 [Norm] toggles between **Norm 1** and **Norm 2**.

- Choosing F1 [Fix] allows you to choose the number of decimal places from 0 to 9 with the calculator rounding to that number of places (That is, choosing **fix 0** displays answers rounded to the nearest whole number).

- Press EXIT to return to the home screen.

Evaluate 1 ÷ 20.

Enter **1** ÷ **20** EXE. DISPLAY: *0.05* Depress the left arrow key. DISPLAY: *1 ÷ 20_* Now you can edit the expression. Change the expression to 1 ÷ 200 and EXE. In **Norm 1** the display will be *5.E-03*. In **Norm 2** the display will be *0.005*.

NOTE: Hitting the right arrow key will allow you to edit the previous expression extreme right to left.

SET UP in the GRAPH Mode

- To access the **GRAPH Mode**, press MENU 5 [GRAPH]. To access **SET UP**, press SHIFT MENU [SET UP]. Scroll down to see all entries in the menu.

  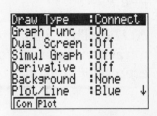

- Check to see that **Background** is **None** and all other settings match the ones shown at the right.

- Return to the **MAIN MENU**: EXIT MENU .

MEM Mode

- If you encounter a **MEM ERROR** message, you will need to free up the memory. Choose ALPHA TAN [MEM] from the **MAIN MENU**.

- Press EXE to display the memory status screen.

- Use the up and down arrows to view the amount of memory (in bytes) used for storage of each type of data.

Clear memory content of a specific data type.

Highlight the data type you want to clear. Press **DEL** F1 **YES** F1 EXIT MENU.

Fraction to Decimal Key

- In the **RUN Mode**, the F↔D key converts fractional answers to decimals and vice versa. If this key does not function, got to the **LINK Mode** at the **MAIN MENU** to make sure the **Image Set** is **Off**. If the **Image Set** is **On**, select F6 [IMGE] F1 [OFF].

Fraction Buttons

- In the **RUN Mode** fractions are entered using the ab/c key. The screen at the right shows how a fraction like $2\frac{3}{4}$ appears on screen.

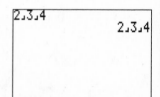

Enter $2\frac{3}{4}$. Find its decimal equivalent and rewrite the number in improper form.

Use the ab/c key after each part of the number. Press **2** ab/c **3** ab/c **4.** F↔D EXE converts the fraction to the decimal equivalent, 2.75. SHIFT ab/c [d/c] EXE converts the fraction or decimal to the improper form $\frac{11}{4}$.

NOTE: This calculator *will not* take a decimal entry and convert it to a fraction. In order to have a fractional answer appear, *the original expression must be entered in fractional form.*

Introduction to the CASIO CFX-9850Ga PLUS
Graphics Calculator (continued)

Basic Calculations

- To enter basic calculations on the *CASIO 9850Ga PLUS* graphics calculator, first select the **RUN Mode** from the **MAIN MENU** screen.

- The following examples show how expressions are entered and the resulting display.

Expression	Keystrokes	Display
$3 + 4 + -2$	**3** [+] **4** [+] [(−)] **2** [EXE]	5
$3 - 8(2)$	**3** [−] **8** [(] **2** [)] [EXE]	-13
3^2	**3** [x^2] [EXE]	9
-3^2	[(−)] **3** [x^2] [EXE]	-9
$(-3)^2$	[(] [(−)] **3** [)] [x^2] [EXE]	9
$\sqrt{20}$	[SHIFT] [x^2] [√] **20** [EXE]	4.472135955
$\sqrt{-2}$	[SHIFT] [x^2] [√] [(−)] **2** [EXE]	1.4142135562i
$\|-4\|$	[OPTN] [F3] [CPLX] [F2] [AbS] [(−)] **4** [EXE] [EXIT] [EXIT]	4
2^3	**2** [△] **3** [EXE]	8
$8!$	**8** [OPTN] [F6] [▷] [F3] [PROB] [F1] [x!] [EXE] [EXIT] [EXIT]	40320
$\sin 45°$	(Make sure **SET UP Mode** is set for **Angle: Deg.**) [sin] **45** [EXE]	0.7071067812

Boolean Logic

- The following examples demonstrate the use of Boolean logic to test relational operations. If the relational operation is true, a "1" will be displayed. If the relational operation is false, a "0" is displayed.

Expression	Keystrokes	Display
$2 < 3$	**2** [SHIFT] [VARS] [F6] [▷] [F3] [REL] [F4] [<] **3** [EXE] [EXIT] [EXIT]	1 (true)
$-6 \geq -5$	[(−)] **6** [SHIFT] [VARS] [F6] [▷] [F3] [REL] [F5] [≥] [(−)] **5** [EXE] [EXIT] [EXIT]	0 (false)

Algebra 1 Graphing Calculator Activities

Introduction to the Texas Instruments TI-83 Graphing Calculator

This section provides helpful hints and specific information about using the TI-83 calculator. If you own a TI-82 calculator, you may find that you need different keystrokes than those provided in this booklet. Refer to your TI-82 Guidebook for the keying sequence you need to perform the same functions.

Setting Preferences

- It is essential to make sure everyone's calculator is set up the same. Always check the following calculator functions: **Y=**, **STAT PLOT**, **FORMAT**, **WINDOW**, and **STAT** before all activities.

NOTE: The name of the function accessed by the 2nd key or the ALPHA key will appear in brackets after the key used to access the function.

Clearing Graphs and Lists

Clearing Equations

- To clear all existing equations **Y=** window, press Y=. Highlight the equation and press CLEAR. Repeat as necessary.

Clearing Statistical Graphs

- To clear any statistical plots from the graph screen, press 2nd Y= to open the **STAT PLOT** window. Select **4:PlotsOff** ENTER. **Done** will appear on the screen.

Clearing Lists

STAT accesses the statistics menu. Selecting **5:SetUpEditor** reorders all lists L1 - L6. To clear all lists you have three options.

1. 2nd 0 [CATALOG]. Scroll down until you see **ClrAllLists** and press ENTER ENTER. **Done** appears on the **Home Screen**.

2. 2nd + [MEM]. Select **4:ClrAllLists** and press ENTER. **Done** appears on the **Home Screen**.

3. STAT 4:ClrList 2nd 1 [L1] , 2nd 2 [L2] , 2nd 3 [L3] , 2nd 4 [L4] , 2nd 5 [L5] , 2nd 6 [L6] ENTER. **Done** appears on the **Home Screen**.

Clearing Drawings

- It may be necessary to clear any drawings. Select 2nd PRGM [DRAW]. Choose **1:ClrDraw** and press ENTER. **Done** appears on the **Home Screen**.

Setting Format Preferences

- 2nd ZOOM allows you to view the **FORMAT** window. It is your option to display the **LabelOff** or **LabelOn** and **ExprOn** or **ExprOff**. **LabelOn** labels the *x*- and *y*-axes in the **TRACE** mode. **ExprOn** displays the equation on the screen in the **TRACE** mode.

Setting the Viewing Window

- Press the WINDOW button. If you need to reset the window, you can manually enter the coordinates for coordinate grid range you desire.

- You can also select ZOOM for alternate choices. Frequently used choices are:

  6:ZStandard   Displays the standard coordinate window [−10, 10] by [−10, 10].

  5:ZSquare   Displays a window in which each unit has the same visual dimension. Graphs in this window resemble those done on grid paper.

Other Features

- **Redisplaying Last Entry** You can redisplay your last entry for editing by pressing 2nd ENTER **[ENTRY]**. Then use the arrow keys to reposition the cursor and edit the entry. The calculator types over the current entries as you enter the new entries. To add to the current entry without typing over, use 2nd DEL **[INS]**.

- **Returning to Home Screen** 2nd MODE **[QUIT]** returns you to the **Home Screen**.

- **Finding a Command** 2nd 0 **[CATALOG]** provides an alphabetical listing of commands that can be entered directly to the home screen.

Memory

- Pressing 2nd + **[MEM]** accesses the memory menu (shown at the right).

- If you encounter memory errors, first look at **1:Check RAM**. Determine where you can free up some memory.

- Press 2nd MODE **[QUIT]** to return to the **Home Screen**.

- Press 2nd + [MEM] and select **2:Delete**.... This provides you with choices to clear. Select the category to clear specific items.

- 2nd MODE [QUIT] returns you to the **Home Screen**.

Fractions and Decimals

- Converting between fractions and decimals requires you to use the MATH button.

- Mixed numbers are written as the sum of a number and a quotient.

- To find the decimal equivalent of $\frac{2}{5}$, enter **2** ÷ **5** MATH and select **2:▷Dec** ENTER. You can also find a decimal value by pressing **2** ÷ **5** ENTER.

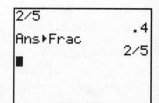

- To change 0.4 back to a fraction, press MATH, select **1:▷Frac**, and press MATH.

NOTE: To convert a decimal to a fraction does not require the original problem to be entered in fraction form. For example, if you enter 2.875, press MATH, select **1:▷Frac**, and press ENTER, the value *23/8* appears. This is the improper form $\frac{23}{8}$ of $2\frac{7}{8}$. The TI-83 will not display a mixed number.

Introduction to the Texas Instruments TI-83 Graphing Calculator (continued)

Basic Calculations

- Enter basic calculations on the TI-83 graphing calculator **Home Screen**.

Expression	Keystrokes	Display
$3 + 4 + -2$	**3** + **4** + (−) **2** ENTER	5
$3 - 8(2)$	**3** − **8** (**2**) ENTER	-13
3^2	**3** x^2 ENTER	9
-3^2	(−) **3** x^2 ENTER	-9
$(-3)^2$	((−) **3**) x^2 ENTER	9
$\sqrt{20}$	2nd x^2 [√] **20**) ENTER	4.472135955
$\sqrt{-2}$	SHIFT x^2 [√] (−) **2**) ENTER	ERR:NONREAL ANS 1∎Quit 2:Goto
$\lvert -4 \rvert$	MATH ▶ [NUM] (select) **1:abs(** (−) **4**) ENTER	4
2^3	**2** ∧ **3** ENTER	8
$8!$	**8** MATH ▶ ▶ ▶ [PRE] (select) **4:!** ENTER	40320
$\sin 45°$	(Make sure MODE is set for **Degree**). sin **45** ENTER OR sin **45** 2nd MATRX [ANGLE] (select) **1:°**) ENTER	0.7071067812

Boolean Logic

- The following examples demonstrate the use of Boolean logic to test relational operations. If the relational operation is true, a "1" will be displayed. If the relational operation is false, a "0" is displayed.

Expression	Keystrokes	Display
$2 < 3$	**2** 2nd MATRX [TEST] (select) **5:< 3** ENTER	1 (true)
$-6 \geq -5$	(−) **6** 2nd MATH [TEST] (select) **4:≥** (−) **5** ENTER	0 (false)

© Glencoe/McGraw-Hill　　　　9　　　　*Algebra 1 Graphing Calculator Activities*

Solving Linear Inequalities in One Variable

Objective   The student will solve linear inequalities in one variable and apply these skills to solve practical problems. Graphing calculators will be used to confirm algebraic solutions.

Use with GLENCOE Algebra 1: Integration, Applications, and Connections		
Lesson	**Lesson Title**	**Student Edition Pages**
7-1	Solving Inequalities by Using Addition and Subtraction	384-390
7-2	Solving Inequalities by Using Multiplication and Division	392-398
7-3	Solving Multi-Step Inequalities	399-404

Hints

- Each calculator has particular protocols with certain procedures. You may find it helpful to practice each lesson before teaching it.

- Relational operator signs are defined as < (is less than), ≤ (is less than or equal to), > (is greater than), ≥ (is greater than or equal to), = (is equal to), and ≠ (is not equal to). The following defines how these operators can be accessed.

For the CASIO CFX-9850Ga Plus

Accessing relational operators: At the **MAIN MENU**, select [1] [RUN]. To access the relational operators, press SHIFT VARS F6 [▷] F3 [REL].

Relational operators are displayed at the bottom of the window. Choose the appropriate symbol using the soft keys (F1 through F6 .)

The symbols stay displayed for use.

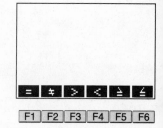

Graphing: Graphical representation of one variable inequalities must be done with paper and pencil.

For the TI-83

Accessing relational operators: To access relational operators from the **Home Screen**, press 2nd MATH and make sure **TEST** is highlighted. Then select a symbol by highlighting the symbol and pressing ENTER or by pressing the associated number key (1 through 6). This procedure must be repeated each time that a symbol is needed.

Graphing:

- Before graphing, first check the calculator settings. Press WINDOW ZOOM and select **6:Zstandard** to set the standard viewing window. To enter an inequality, press Y= . Use arrow keys to highlight any existing equations and press CLEAR to remove any previously entered data.

- To enter the inequality $x < 6$ enter X,T,θ,n 2nd MATH [TEST], select **5: <**, and enter **6.** Then press GRAPH . A screen similar to the one at the right should appear.

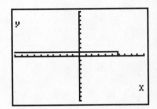

  Press ZOOM and select **4:ZDecimal** to get a closer look at the inequality. You will need to press TRACE to move the cursor to $x = 5.9$ and $y = 1$.

- The calculator uses Boolean logic to display the graph. When $y = 1$, the x values shown are part of the solution set as shown in Figure 1. When $y = 0$, the x values shown are *not* part of the solution set as shown in Figure 2.

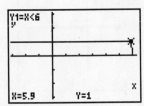

Figure 1

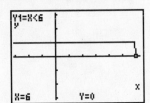

Figure 2

Therefore, the range value of 1 indicates all x values that are solutions to $x < 6$.

Graphing Calculator Activity 1 (continued)
TEACHING SUGGESTIONS

Answers for Student Worksheet Practice

Boundary Point	Solution	Graph	Sample Graph (TI-83)
1. $\frac{2}{5}$ or 0.4	$\left\{ x \mid x \geq \frac{2}{5} \right\}$		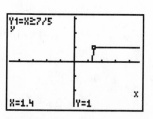
2. $\frac{7}{5}$ or 1.4	$\left\{ x \mid x \geq \frac{7}{5} \right\}$	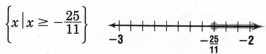	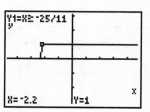
3. $-\frac{25}{11}$ or $-2.\overline{27}$	$\left\{ x \mid x \geq -\frac{25}{11} \right\}$		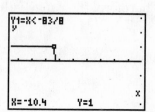
4. -10.375	$\{ x \mid x < -10.375 \}$ or $\left\{ x \mid x < -\frac{83}{8} \right\}$		
5. $\frac{8}{13} \approx 0.61538462$	$\left\{ x \mid x < \frac{8}{13} \right\}$	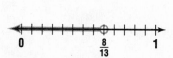	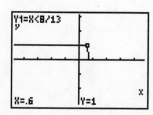

Graphing Calculator Activity 1

Solving Linear Inequalities in One Variable

You can use the graphing calculator to solve an inequality and to check your solution.

Solve $x + \frac{1}{8} < \frac{1}{2}$ and check your solution. Then graph your solution.

- From the **MAIN MENU**, press **1** [RUN] to go to **RUN MODE**. Enter the inequality.

  Enter: X,θ,T + 1 a^b/c 8 SHIFT VARS F6 [▷] F3 [REL]
  F4 [<] 1 a^b/c 2 EXE

- To solve the equation, you need to add the inverse of $\frac{1}{8}$ to each side of the inequality. Instead of paper and pencil, you will use the calculator screen to record the steps in solving the inequality. The calculator does *not* solve it for you.

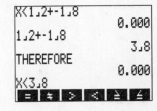

```
X+1⌐8<1⌐2
                0.000
X+1⌐8+-1⌐8<1⌐2+-1⌐8
                0.000
X<1⌐2+-1⌐8
                0.000
```

NOTE: The *0.000* display indicates that the calculator is using Boolean logic to test relational operations. If an operation is true, a "1" is displayed. If it is false, a "0" is displayed. During this exercise, ignore the Boolean logic results of 1 or 0 until the check of the boundary value.

- Use the following keystrokes to add $\frac{1}{2} + \left(-\frac{1}{8}\right)$.

  Enter: 1 a^b/c **2** + (−) **1** a^b/c **8** EXE

  The answer is $\frac{3}{8}$.

```
X<1⌐2+-1⌐8
                0.000
1⌐2+-1⌐8
                 3⌐8
THEREFORE
                0.000
X<3⌐8
```

  Hint: To display "THEREFORE" on the screen, select SHIFT ALPHA [A-LOCK] and type in the letters located on the top right of the keys.

- Store this answer as the *x* value.

  Enter: SHIFT (−) [Ans] → X,θ,T EXE

  You have stored the boundary value of the inequality.

- You can check the boundary value by replacing the inequality sign with an equal sign and checking the equation. Press AC/ON and the up arrow key until the original inequality $x + \frac{1}{8} < \frac{1}{2}$ appears. Press the right arrow key until < is highlighted. Press SHIFT · [=] EXE to replace the inequality sign with an equal sign. A *l* will appear, showing that the boundary value you stored as the *x* value is the solution to the equation. (A zero would indicate that the number is not the solution.)

- Make a line graph to show the solution set of the inequality. Label the solution set $\left\{x \mid x < \frac{3}{8}\right\}$.

Graphing Calculator Activity 1

Solving Linear Inequalities in One Variable

You can use the graphing calculator to solve an inequality and to check your solution.

Solve $x + \frac{1}{8} < \frac{1}{2}$ and check your solution. Then graph your solution.

- First set the calculator to round decimal answers to three places by pressing MODE and using the arrow keys to move down to **FLOAT** and across to **3**. Press ENTER.

- Return to the **Home Screen**, and enter the inequality.

  Enter: X,T,θ,n   +   1   ÷   8   2nd   MATH   [TEST] **5** (to select <) **1**   ÷   **2**   ENTER

- To solve the equation, you need to add the inverse of $\frac{1}{8}$ to each side of the inequality. Instead of paper and pencil, you will use the calculator screen to record the steps in solving the inequality. The calculator does *not* solve it for you.

```
X+1/8<1/2
            0.000
X+1/8+-1/8<1/2+-
1/8
            0.000
X<1/2+-1/8
            0.000
■
```

NOTE: The *0.000* display indicates that the calculator is using Boolean logic to test relational operations. If an operation is true, a "1" is displayed. If it is false, a "0" is displayed. During this exercise, ignore the Boolean logic results of 1 or 0 until the check of the boundary value.

- Use the following keystrokes to add $\frac{1}{2} + \left(-\frac{1}{8}\right)$.

  Enter: 1   ÷   2   +   (−)   1   ÷   8   ENTER

  The answer is shown as a decimal. To change the answer to a fraction, press MATH ENTER ENTER. The answer is $\frac{3}{8}$.

```
1/2+-1/8
            .375
Ans▶Frac
            3/8
THEREFORE
            0.000
X<3/8
```

  Hint: To display "THEREFORE" on the screen, select 2nd ALPHA **[A-LOCK]** and type in the letters located on the top right of the keys.

- Store this answer as the x value.

  Enter: 3   ÷   8   STO▶   X,T,θ,n   ENTER

  You have stored the boundary value of the inequality.

- You can check the boundary value by replacing the inequality sign with an equal sign and checking the equation. Press [2nd] [ENTER] [TEST] and repeat this procedure until the original inequality $x + \frac{1}{8} < \frac{1}{2}$ appears. Press the left arrow key until < is highlighted. Press [2nd] [MATH] [TEST] [ENTER] to replace the inequality sign with an equal sign. Press [ENTER] again and 1.000 will appear. This one indicates that the number you stored as the x value is the solution to the equation. (A zero would indicate that the number is not the solution.)

- Make a line graph to show the solution set of the inequality. Label the solution set $\left\{ x \mid x < \frac{3}{8} \right\}$.

- Use the graphing calculator to verify your line graph. First press [ZOOM] and select **6:ZStandard**. Then press [Y=], highlight each existing equation, and press [CLEAR]. Once you have deleted all existing equations, highlight \Y1= and enter the inequality.

  Enter: [X,T,θ,n] [2nd] [MATH] [TEST] **5** (to select <) **3** [÷] **8** [GRAPH]

NOTE: Boolean logic is used to represent the solution set. All x values paired with y values of 1 make the inequality true, and all x values paired with y values of 0 make the inequality false.

- Press [TRACE] and use the arrow keys to place the cursor where the graph turns downward to $y = 0$. For a closer look, press [ZOOM], select **2:Zoom In**, and press [ENTER].

- Press [TRACE] and explore which values belong to the solution set and which values do not belong to the solution set.

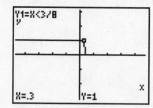

Graphing Calculator Activity 1

Solving Linear Inequalities in One Variable

Practice

Solve each inequality. Name the boundary point. Graph and label the solution set. Use the graphing calculator to verify your work.

1. $10x - 2 \geq 5x$

Graph:

Boundary point:_____

Solution set: _____

2. $2x + \frac{3}{5} \leq 3x - \frac{4}{5}$

Graph:

Boundary point:_____

Solution set: _____

3. $3(x - 6) \leq 14x + 7$

Graph:

Boundary point:_____

Solution set: _____

4. $0.3x - 4 > 0.7x + 0.15$

Graph:

Boundary point:_____

Solution set: _____

5. $0.6(x - 2) + 0.14 \geq 0.7x - 0.26$

Graph:

Boundary point:_____

Solution set: _____

Graphing Calculator Activity 2
TEACHING SUGGESTIONS

Solving Equations with the Variable on Both Sides

Objective   The student will justify steps used in simplifying expressions and solving equations and inequalities. Justifications will include the use of concrete objects, pictorial representations, and the properties of real numbers.

Use with GLENCOE Algebra 1: Integration, Applications, and Connections		
Lesson	**Lesson Title**	**Student Edition Pages**
3-5	Solving Equations with the Variable on Both Sides	168-172

Hints

• The following lesson is only one method for solving linear equations. Students convert each rational expression to a common denominator for the purpose of practicing finding equivalent fractions.

• Each calculator has particular protocols with certain procedures. You may find it helpful to practice each lesson before teaching it.

For the CASIO CFX-9850Ga PLUS

You can use the equation solver feature to solve a given equation.

Example: Solve $\frac{2x-3}{6} = \frac{2x}{3} + \frac{1}{2}$.

• From **MAIN MENU** choose **EQUA** by pressing ⟨ALPHA⟩ ⟨X,θ,T⟩ **[A]** ⟨F3⟩ **[SOLV]**. Highlight **Eq:** and press the following sequence of keys:

⟨(⟩ 2 ⟨X,θ,T⟩ ⟨−⟩ 3 ⟨)⟩ ⟨ab/c⟩ 6 ⟨SHIFT⟩ ⟨·⟩ **[=]** 2 ⟨X,θ,T⟩ ⟨ab/c⟩ 3 ⟨+⟩ 1 ⟨ab/c⟩ 2 ⟨EXE⟩ ⟨EXE⟩

Ignore any existing equations.

NOTE: If you press ⟨F6⟩ **[SOLV]** after entering the equation, you will get the same result.

• The answer, −3, is displayed along with the left side and right side check results.

• Pressing ⟨F1⟩ **[REPT]** returns you to the original screen. Press ⟨MENU⟩ 1 **[RUN]**.

```
Eq:(2X-3).6=2X.3+1.2
   X=-3.000
Lft=-1.500
Rgt=-1.500


REPT
```

NOTE: The screen shows values with three decimal places because the **Display** menu under **SET UP** has been set to **Fix3**. See instructions in the *Introduction to the CASIO CFX-9850Ga PLUS Graphics Calculator* on page 3 to change the number of decimal places displayed.

Graphing Calculator Activity 2 (continued)
TEACHING SUGGESTIONS

- Students will now enter the equation in the **RUN MODE** using the same keystrokes as before. After an equation is entered, press EXE and the calculator will respond with a "1". This shows that the calculator value for x that was found in the equation solver is the true solution to this equation.

  The calculator uses Boolean logic to test for equality. A "1" means a true statement. A "0" means a false statement.

- Students will type the solution steps on the calculator and press EXE after each step.

- You can verify the student's work by pressing AC/ON ▲. Continue to scroll upward to see the steps entered on the calculator.

For the TI-83

You can use the equation solver feature to solve a given equation.

Example: Solve $\frac{2x-3}{6} = \frac{2x}{3} + \frac{1}{2}$.

- From the **Home Screen** choose MATH. Press the down arrow key until you see **0:Solver.** *If there is an equation present, the calculator takes you to the solution screen. Press the up arrow once for the equation solver screen. Then press* CLEAR. *The up and down arrows toggle you back and forth between the equation solver screen and the solution screen.*

- The equation must be set equal to zero before it is input into the calculator.
  $$\frac{2x-3}{6} - \frac{2x}{3} - \frac{1}{2} = 0$$

- Input the equation using the following keystrokes:
  (2 X,T,θ,n − 3) ÷ 6 − 2 X,T,θ,n ÷ 3 − 1 ÷ 2 ENTER

- The screen should look like the one at the right. Note that x will equal zero or the last calculated x value, not necessarily the solution for the entered equation.

```
(2X-3)/6-2X/3...=0
X=0
bound={-1E99, 1...
```

- Highlight **X =**, and press ALPHA ENTER [SOLVE]. The answer is displayed.

Important:
When fractions are used in the original equation you may get a repeating decimal answer, such as $X = -2.99999$. To round this number, highlight **X** and enter the rounded number. Then solve again. Press ALPHA ENTER [SOLVE]. If your rounded answer is correct, the screen shows **left − rt = 0**. The value −3 is stored as **X**.

- To return to the **HOME SCREEN**, press 2nd MODE [QUIT].

Graphing Calculator Activity 2 (continued)
TEACHING SUGGESTIONS

- Now enter the original equation:

  (2 [X,T,θ,*n*] − 3) ÷ 6 [2nd] [MATH] . Select **1: =**. Then press **2** [X,T,θ,*n*] ÷ 3 + 1 ÷ 2 [ENTER]

  The screen displays 1. This shows that the value for x found in the **EQUATION SOLVER** is the true solution to this equation.

  The calculator uses Boolean logic to test for equality. A "1" means a true statement. A "0" means a false statement.

- Students will then type the solution steps on the calculator and [ENTER] after each step. A "1" will verify a correct step. A "0" will indicate an error has been made.

- You can verify the student's work by repeatedly pressing [2nd] [ENTER] **[ENTRY]**.

Answers for Student Worksheet Practice

1. $x = 10$
2. $n = -16$
3. $y = -3$
4. $b = 8$
5. $x = 2$

Graphing Calculator Activity 2

Solving Equations with the Variable on Both Sides

You can use the equation solver function on the graphing calculator to solve multi-step equations with variables on both sides of the equation. You can also use the graphing calculator to check each step used to solve an equation.

Use the graphing calculator to solve $\frac{2x-3}{6} = \frac{2x}{3} + \frac{1}{2}$.

- First delete all existing equations. From the **MAIN MENU**, press
  `ALPHA` `X,T,θ,n` [A] [EQUA] `F3` [SOLV] `F2` [DEL] `F1` [YES].

- Input the equation. If more than one term is in the numerator, place terms in parentheses.

  Enter: `(` 2 `X,T,θ,n` `−` 3 `)` `ab/c` 6 `SHIFT` `·` [=] 2 `X,θ,T`
  `ab/c` 3 `+` 1 `ab/c` 2 `EXE`

  X = will be highlighted. An earlier stored value for x may be displayed. This may not be the solution. Press `F6` **[SOLV]**. $X = -3$ will be displayed along with the values obtained when -3 is substituted for x in the left and right sides of the equation. Since the left side equals the right side, the equation checks.

  ```
  Eq:(2X-3)⌐6=2X⌐3+1⌐2
    X=-3.000
  Lft=-1.500
  Rgt=-1.500


  REPT
  ```

NOTE: Make sure that **Display** in the **SET UP** is set for **Fix3** (3 decimal places).

- `F1` **[REPT]** takes you back to the original equation. The up arrow ▲ and right arrow ► keys allow you to edit the original equation.

- Return to the **RUN MODE** by pressing `MENU` 1 **[RUN]**. Solve the original equation showing all steps. Press `EXE` after each step. If you have correctly entered the steps, a "1" will be displayed. A "0" will be displayed if your steps are incorrect.

Graphing Calculator Activity 2 (continued)

Solve $\dfrac{2x-3}{6} = \dfrac{2x}{3} + \dfrac{1}{2}$. **Use the graphing calculator to verify each step.**

Paper and Pencil	Calculator
• Write the equation. $\dfrac{2x-3}{6} = \dfrac{2x}{3} + \dfrac{1}{2}$	• **Enter:** ⎣(⎦ **2** ⎣X,θ,T⎦ ⎣−⎦ **3** ⎣)⎦ ⎣aᵇ/c⎦ **6** ⎣SHIFT⎦ ⎣·⎦ [=] **2** ⎣X,θ,T⎦ ⎣aᵇ/c⎦ **3** ⎣+⎦ **1** ⎣aᵇ/c⎦ **2** ⎣EXE⎦ *I* appears.
• Multiply all terms by the LCM of the denominators, which is 6. Simplify. $6\left(\dfrac{2x-3}{6}\right) = 6\left(\dfrac{2x}{3}\right) + 6\left(\dfrac{1}{2}\right)$	• **Enter: 6** ⎣(⎦ ⎣(⎦ **2** ⎣X,θ,T⎦ ⎣−⎦ **3** ⎣)⎦ ⎣aᵇ/c⎦ **6** ⎣)⎦ ⎣SHIFT⎦ ⎣·⎦ [=] **6** ⎣(⎦ **2** ⎣X,θ,T⎦ ⎣aᵇ/c⎦ **3** ⎣)⎦ ⎣+⎦ **6** ⎣(⎦ **1** ⎣aᵇ/c⎦ **2** ⎣)⎦ ⎣EXE⎦ *I* appears showing this is correct.
• Simplify the equality. $2x - 3 = 4x + 3$	• **Enter: 2** ⎣X,θ,T⎦ ⎣−⎦ **3** ⎣SHIFT⎦ ⎣·⎦ [=] **4** ⎣X,θ,T⎦ ⎣+⎦ **3** ⎣EXE⎦ *I* appears showing this is correct.
• Add the additive inverse of $2x$ to each side. $-2x + 2x - 3 = -2x + 4x + 3$	• **Enter:** ⎣(−)⎦ **2** ⎣X,θ,T⎦ ⎣+⎦ **2** ⎣X,θ,T⎦ ⎣−⎦ **3** ⎣SHIFT⎦ ⎣·⎦ [=] ⎣(−)⎦ **2** ⎣X,θ,T⎦ ⎣+⎦ **4** ⎣X,θ,T⎦ ⎣+⎦ **3** ⎣EXE⎦ *I* appears showing this is correct.
• Simplify the equality. $-3 = 2x + 3$	• **Enter:** ⎣(−)⎦ **3** ⎣SHIFT⎦ ⎣·⎦ [=] **2** ⎣X,θ,T⎦ ⎣+⎦ **3** ⎣EXE⎦ *I* appears showing this is correct.

Graphing Calculator Activity 2 (continued)

Paper and Pencil	Calculator
• Add the additive inverse of 3 to each side. $-3 + (-3) = -3 + 2x + 3$	• **Enter:** (−) 3 + (−) 3 SHIFT · [=] (−) 3 + 2 X,θ,T + 3 EXE *I* appears showing this is correct.
• Simplify the equality. $-6 = 2x$	• **Enter:** (−) 6 SHIFT · [=] 2 X,θ,T EXE *I* appears showing this is correct.
• Multiply each side by the multiplicative inverse of 2. $\frac{1}{2}(-6) = \frac{1}{2}(2x)$	• **Enter:** 1 a^b/c 2 × (−) 6 SHIFT · [=] 1 a^b/c 2 × 2 X,θ,T EXE *I* appears showing this is correct.
• Simplify the equality. $-3 = x$	• **Enter:** (−) 3 SHIFT · [=] X,θ,T EXE *I* appears showing this is correct.

You have now solved the equation step by step, verifying each step.

Graphing Calculator Activity 2

Solving Equations with the Variable on Both Sides

You can use the equation solver function on the graphing calculator to solve multi-step equations with variables on both sides of the equation. You can also use the graphing calculator to check each step used to solve an equation.

Use the graphing calculator to solve $\frac{2x-3}{6} = \frac{2x}{3} + \frac{1}{2}$.

- First delete all existing equations. From the **Home Screen** press MATH , and use the down arrow to find **0:Solver**. Press ENTER . If there is an equation present, the calculator takes you to the solution screen. Press the up arrow once to see the **EQUATION SOLVER** screen. Press CLEAR . The up/down arrows will change the screen back and forth between the **EQUATION SOLVER** screen and the solution screen.

- Before you can enter the equation into the calculator, you must rewrite the equation so that one side equals 0.

$$\frac{2x-3}{6} - \frac{2x}{3} - \frac{1}{2} = 0$$

- Input the equation.

Enter: (2 X,T,θ,n − 3) ÷ 6 − 2 X,T,θ,n ÷ 3 − 1 ÷ 2 ENTER

```
(2X-3)/6-2X/3...=0
X=0
bound={-1E99,1...
```

Notice that x will equal zero or the last calculated x value, not necessarily the solution for the entered equation.

- To find the solution of the equation, highlight **X=** and press ALPHA ENTER **[SOLVE]**. The answer will appear.

NOTE: When fractions are used in the original equation, you may get a repeating decimal answer such as $x = -2.99999$. Round this number. Highlight **X=** and enter the rounded number. Press ALPHA ENTER **[SOLVE]**. If your rounded answer is correct, the screen shows **left − rt = 0**. The value -3 is stored as x.

- To return to **Home Screen**, press 2nd MODE **[QUIT]**.

Solve $\frac{2x-3}{6} = \frac{2x}{3} + \frac{1}{2}$. **Use the graphing calculator to verify each step.**

Paper and Pencil	Calculator
• Write the equation. $$\frac{2x-3}{6} = \frac{2x}{3} + \frac{1}{2}$$	• **Enter:** (2 X,θ,T − 3) ÷ 6 2nd MATH [TEST] **1** (to select =) **2** X,θ,T ÷ 3 + **1** ÷ **2** ENTER *1.000* appears.
• Multiply all terms by the LCM of the denominators, which is 6. $$6\left(\frac{2x-3}{6}\right) = 6\left(\frac{2x}{3}\right) + 6\left(\frac{1}{2}\right)$$	• **Enter: 6** ((2 X,T,θ,n − 3) ÷ 6) 2nd MATH [TEST] **1** (to select =) **6** (2 X,T,θ,n ÷ 3) + 6 (1 ÷ 2) ENTER *1.000* appears showing this is correct.
• Simplify the equality. $$2x - 3 = 4x + 3$$	• **Enter: 2** X,T,θ,n − 3 2nd MATH [TEST] **1** (to select =) **4** X,T,θ,n + 3 ENTER *1.000* appears showing this is correct.
• Add the additive inverse of $2x$ to each side. $$-2x + 2x - 3 = -2x + 4x + 3$$	• **Enter:** (−) 2 X,T,θ,n + 2 X,T,θ,n − 3 2nd MATH [TEST] **1** (to select =) (−) 2 X,T,θ,n + 4 X,T,θ,n + 3 ENTER *1.000* appears showing this is correct.
• Simplify the equality. $$-3 = 2x + 3$$	• **Enter:** (−) 3 2nd MATH [TEST] **1** (to select =) 2 X,T,θ,n + 3 ENTER *1.000* appears showing this is correct.

Graphing Calculator Activity 2 (continued)   TI-83 Keystrokes

- Add the additive inverse of 3 to each side.

  $-3 + (-3) = -3 + 2x + 3$

- **Enter:** (-) 3 + (-) 3 2nd MATH [TEST] 1 (to select =) (-) 3 + 2 X,T,θ,n + 3 ENTER

  1.000 appears showing this is correct.

- Simplify the equality.

  $-6 = 2x$

- **Enter:** (-) 6 2nd MATH [TEST] 1 (to select =) 2 X,T,θ,n ENTER

  1.000 appears showing this is correct.

- Multiply each side by the multiplicative inverse of 2.

  $\frac{1}{2}(-6) = \frac{1}{2}(2x)$

- **Enter:** 1 ÷ 2 × (-) 6 2nd MATH [TEST] 1 (to select =) 1 ÷ 2 × 2 X,T,θ,n ENTER

  1.000 appears showing this is correct.

- Simplify the equality.

  $-3 = x$

- **Enter:** (-) 3 2nd MATH [TEST] 1 (to select =) X,T,θ,n ENTER

  1.000 appears showing this is correct.

You have now solved the equation step by step, verifying each step.

Graphing Calculator Activity 2

Solving Equations with the Variable on Both Sides

Practice

Solve the following equations verifying each step with the graphing calculator.

1. $6x + 7 = 8x - 13$

2. $\frac{3}{4}n + 16 = 2 - \frac{1}{8}n$

3. $6(y + 2) - 4 = -10$

4. $5 - \frac{1}{2}(b - 6) = 4$

5. $2(x - 3) + 5 = 3(x - 1)$

Graphing Calculator Activity 3
TEACHING SUGGESTIONS

Basic Matrix Operations:
Addition, Subtraction, and Scalar Multiplication

Objective   The student will use matrices to organize and manipulate data, including matrix addition, subtraction, and scalar multiplication.

Use with GLENCOE Algebra 1: Integration, Applications, and Connections		
Lesson	Lesson Title	Student Edition Pages
2-3	Adding and Subtracting Integers	85-92
2-5	Adding and Subtracting Rational Numbers	100-104
2-6	Multiplying Rational Numbers	106-111

Hints

- Each calculator has particular protocols with certain procedures. You may find it helpful to practice each lesson before teaching it.

For the CASIO GFX-9850Ga PLUS

Defining a Matrix   You define matrices using the **MAT MODE**.

Matrix Operations

- You perform all matrix operations (addition, subtraction, scalar multiplication) in the **RUN MODE**, using OPTN F2 [MAT].

- To enter the product of 2 and matrix A, you can enter any of the following. **Mat A** indicates matrix A.

  2 Mat A   2 × Mat A   Mat A × 2

  If **Mat A2** is entered, a **Syn ERROR** message appears meaning a syntax error has occurred.

- When adding or subtracting matrices, the matrices must be the same size. If the two matrices are not the same size, **a Dim ERROR** message appears meaning the dimensions of the two matrices do not match. Press AC/ON to clear the error message. Return to the **MAT MODE** to correct the dimension error.

NOTE: The **Dim ERROR** message will also appear if you enter a matrix name that has not been defined yet.

- To enter the product of a negative number and a matrix, the negative number must be enclosed in parentheses or a **MaERROR** will appear. That is, the product of −2 and matrix A should be entered as **(−2) Mat A**. Press AC/ON to clear the error message.

For the TI-83

Defining a matrix You define matrices accessing the matrix menu with the MATRX key.

Matrix Operations

- To perform operations with matrices (addition, subtraction, scalar multiplication), you enter them as if you were entering a numerical expression. To select a matrix to enter in the expression, press the MATRX key, and highlight the matrix you want to use.

- To enter the product of 2 and matrix A, you can enter any of the following. [A] indicates matrix A.

  2[A]   [A]2   2 × [A]   [A] × 2

- When adding or subtracting matrices, the matrices must be the same size. If the two matrices are not the same size, an error message is displayed.
  ERR: DIM MISMATCH
  1: Quit
  2: Goto
  Select **2:Goto** to return to the home screen and the blinking cursor will designate where the error occurred. You can correct the dimension errors using the MATRX key.

- If you reference a matrix that has not been defined, the following message appears.
  ERR: UNDEFINED
  1: Quit
  2: Goto
  Select **2:Goto** to return to the home screen where the cursor blinks to the right of the undefined matrix.

Answers for Student Worksheet

Practice

CASIO CFX-9850Ga PLUS

TI-83

1.
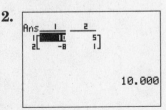

1.
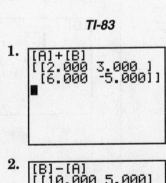

2.
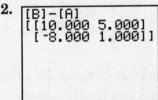

2.

Algebra 1 Graphing Calculator Activities

Graphing Calculator Activity 3 (continued)
TEACHING SUGGESTIONS

CASIO CFX-9850Ga PLUS   **TI-83**

3.
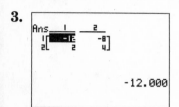

4.
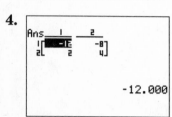
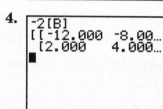

5.
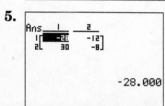
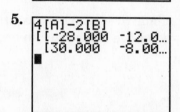

Solutions for Applications

1. Enter shipment 1 as matrix *A*. Enter shipment 2 as matrix *B*. Add matrix *A* and matrix *B* to find the total shipment. Store the resulting matrix as matrix *C*.

CASIO CFX-9850Ga PLUS

- Access **RUN MODE**.
- Enter OPTN F2 [MAT] F1 [Mat] ALPHA X,θ,T [A] + F1 [Mat] ALPHA LOG [B] EXE F1 [Mat] SHIFT (−) [ANS] → F1 [Mat] ALPHA In [C] EXE.
- Matrix *C* appears as:

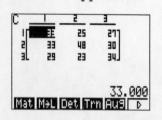

TI-83

- Enter MATRX 1 + MATRX 2 ENTER STO▶ MATRX 3 ENTER
- Display matrix *C* by pressing MATRX 3 ENTER

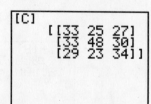

2. Add each cell to find the total number of units shipped. Multiply this sum by $0.27. The answer is $76.14.

3. Create matrix D to represent the required inventory balance. Subtract the total shipment matrix (matrix C) from the required inventory matrix (matrix D). To determine the answer, use the following keystrokes:

CASIO CFX-9850Ga PLUS

- Define matrix D by pressing MENU 3 [MAT]. Highlight **Mat D** and press 3 EXE 3 EXE to set the dimensions.

- Then fill every element in matrix D with the constant 50 by entering MENU 1 [RUN] OPTN F2 [MAT] F6 [▷] F3 [Fill] 50 , F6 [▷] F1 [Mat] ALPHA sin [D]) EXE.

- To view matrix D, select F1 [MAT] ALPHA sin [D] EXE.

- To determine how much is left at the end of the week, find $D - C$, by pressing F1 [Mat] ALPHA sin [D] − F1 [Mat] ALPHA ln [C] EXE. The answer matrix is shown below.

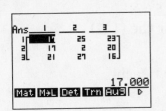

TI-83

- Define matrix D by pressing MATRX . Highlight **EDIT**. Select **4:[D]**. Enter the dimensions by pressing 3 ENTER 3 ENTER.

- To fill every element in matrix D with the constant 50, press MATRX and use the arrow keys to highlight **MATH**. Select **4:Fill(**. Enter 50 , MATRX **4:[D]**) ENTER. The screen will say **Done**.

- To view matrix D, press MATRX and select **4:[D]** ENTER.

- To determine how much is left at the end of the week, find $D - C$, by pressing MATRX **4:[D]** − MATRX **3:[C]** ENTER. The answer matrix is shown below.

```
[D]-[C]
    [[17 25 23]
     [17 2  20]
     [21 27 16]]
```

4. Matrix C provides the total amount of units of ice cream that needs to be replenished.

Algebra 1 Graphing Calculator Activities

Graphing Calculator Activity 3

Basic Matrix Operations:
Addition, Subtraction, and Scalar Multiplication

The graphing calculator can be used to analyze data from business, industry, and consumer situations when the information is presented as matrices. In this activity, you will learn to add matrices, subtract matrices, and perform scalar multiplication using the graphing calculator.

Enter the matrices A $= \begin{bmatrix} 3 & -2 \\ 0 & 5 \end{bmatrix}$ **and B** $= \begin{bmatrix} 12 & -5 \\ -1 & 4 \end{bmatrix}$ **into the graphing calculator.**

- To go to **MATRIX MODE**, press MENU 3 **[MAT]**. If you do not see **None** beside each matrix, press F2 **[DEL-A]** F1 **[YES]**.

- To enter data into a matrix, highlight **Mat A**.

  (*Note:* There are 26 possible matrices.)

- To define the dimensions for matrix *A*, press 2 EXE 2 EXE. The calculator automatically moves into the matrix frame, with the cursor on the first row, first column, or the (1, 1) position.

- Data is recorded left to right, row by row. Press EXE after each entry.

  Enter: 3 EXE (-) **2** EXE **0** EXE **5** EXE

- Press EXIT to return to matrix options.

- Press the down arrow once to highlight **Mat B**.

- To define the dimensions for matrix *B*, press 2 EXE 2 EXE. The cursor again moves to the first row, first column, or the (1, 1) position.

- Enter the data left to right, row by row. Press EXE after each entry.

  Enter: 12 EXE (-) **5** EXE (-) **1** EXE **4** EXE

Now you are ready to perform matrix operations.

Graphing Calculator Activity 3 (continued)

Find A + B.

- Go to **RUN MODE** by pressing EXIT MENU 1 [RUN].

- Now find the sum of matrix A and matrix B.

   Enter: OPTN F2 [MAT] F1 [Mat] ALPHA X,θ,T [A] + F1
   [MAT] ALPHA LOG [B] EXE

   This is the
   Ans (answer) Matrix.

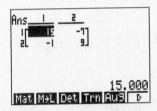

Find A − B.

- Press EXIT EXIT EXIT to display the previous expression
   Mat A + Mat B.

- Press the right arrow key ▶ once. You can now edit the
   expression.

- Press the right arrow key twice to highlight the "+" sign. Press −
   EXE. The difference of matrix A minus matrix B will appear on
   the screen.

   This is the
   Ans Matrix.

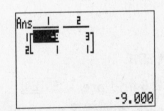

Find 3A − 2B, and store the resulting matrix as C.

- Press EXIT to display the previous expression **Mat A − Mat B.**

- To edit the expression, press the right arrow key once and press
   SHIFT DEL [INS] **3.** Then use the right arrow key to highlight the
   "M" in **Mat B** and press SHIFT DEL [INS] **2** EXE.

   This is the
   Ans Matrix.

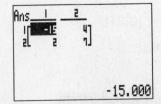

- To store this matrix as C, press OPTN F2 [MAT] F1 [Mat]
   SHIFT (−) [Ans] ➞ F1 [Mat] ALPHA ln [C] EXE.

Basic Matrix Operations:
Addition, Subtraction, and Scalar Multiplication

The graphing calculator can be used to analyze data from business, industry, and consumer situations when the information is presented as matrices. In this activity, you will learn to add matrices, subtract matrices, and perform scalar multiplication using the graphing calculator.

Enter the matrices $A = \begin{bmatrix} 3 & -2 \\ 0 & 5 \end{bmatrix}$ **and** $B = \begin{bmatrix} 12 & -5 \\ -1 & 4 \end{bmatrix}$ **into the graphing calculator.**

- To clear existing matrices, press 2nd + [MEM]. Select **2:Delete** and then select **5:Matrix**. Use the up and down arrow keys to choose the desired matrix and press ENTER until all defined matrices are cleared.

- To define the matrices, press MATRX.

- Move the cursor to the right to highlight **EDIT** and press ENTER.

- To define the dimensions for matrix A, press 2 ENTER 2 ENTER. The cursor moves to the first row, first column or the (1, 1) position.

- Data is recorded left to right, row by row. Press ENTER after each entry.
  Enter: 3 ENTER (−) **2** ENTER **0** ENTER **5** ENTER

- Press MATRX to return to matrix options.

- Move the cursor to the right to highlight **EDIT**.

- Press the down arrow once to highlight **2: B** and press ENTER.

- To define the dimensions for matrix B, press 2 ENTER 2 ENTER. The cursor again moves to the first row, first column or the (1, 1) position.

- Enter the data left to right, row by row. Press ENTER after each entry.
  Enter: 12 ENTER (−) **5** ENTER (−) **1** ENTER **4** ENTER

Now you are ready to perform matrix operations.

Find $A + B$.

- To return to **Home Screen**, press 2nd MODE [QUIT].
- Press MATRX. **1: [A]** 2×2 will be highlighted.
- Press ENTER + MATRX.
- Move the cursor to highlight **2: [B]** 2×2 and press ENTER.

- If you press ENTER again, the sum of matrix *A* and matrix *B* will appear on the screen.

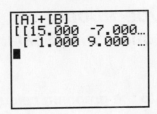

Find A − B.

- Press 2nd ENTER [ENTRY] to display the previous expression [A] + [B].
- Use the left arrow key to highlight the addition sign.
- Press the subtraction key and ENTER. The difference of matrix *A* minus matrix *B* will appear on the screen.

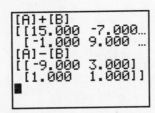

Find 3A − 2B, and store the resulting matrix as C.

- Press 2nd ENTER [ENTRY] to display the previous expression [A] − [B].
- Use the left cursor key to move to the left of the expression.

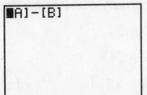

- Press 2nd DEL [INS] 3.
- Press the right cursor twice.

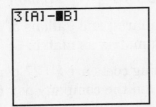

- Press 2nd DEL [INS] 2 ENTER. The answer will appear on the screen.
- To store this matrix as *C*, press 2nd (−) [ANS] MATRX STO▸ 3 (to select [C]) ENTER.

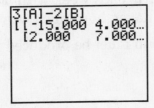

Graphing Calculator Activity 3

Basic Matrix Operations:
Addition, Subtraction, and Scalar Multiplication

Practice

Enter each matrix into the graphing calculator. Then find each sum, difference, or product.

$$A = \begin{bmatrix} -4 & -1 \\ 7 & -3 \end{bmatrix} \qquad B = \begin{bmatrix} 6 & 4 \\ -1 & -2 \end{bmatrix}$$

1. $A + B$

2. $B - A$

3. $3A$

4. $-2B$

5. $4A - 2B$

Applications

An ice cream company makes three flavors of ice cream (munchy chunky, strawnana, and orange delight) in three sizes (pints, quarts, and gallons). The company sent out two shipments this week.

Shipment 1

	MC	S	OD
pint	18	12	15
quart	15	33	14
gallon	16	15	18

Shipment 2

	MC	S	OD
pint	15	13	12
quart	18	15	16
gallon	13	8	16

1. How many pints, quarts, and gallons of each flavor did they ship? Store the resulting matrix as matrix C.

2. The average shipping costs are $0.27 per unit (pint, quart, or gallon). How much money did the company pay for shipping this week?

3. If the company starts each week with 50 pints, 50 quarts, and 50 gallons of each flavor, how much was left at the end of the week?

4. How much ice cream must be produced to replenish the inventory for next Monday?

Graphing Calculator Activity 4
TEACHING SUGGESTIONS

Recognizing Patterns:
Investigating Algebraic Relationships in Regular Polygons

Objective   The student will analyze a given set of data for the existence of a pattern, represent the pattern algebraically and graphically, if possible, and determine if the relation is a function.

Use with GLENCOE Algebra 1: Integration, Applications, and Connections		
Lesson	**Lesson Title**	**Student Edition Pages**
1-2	Patterns and Sequences	12-18
5-6	Writing Equations from Patterns	295-302

Hints

- Each calculator has particular protocols with certain procedures. You may find it helpful to practice each lesson before teaching it.

For the CASIO CFX-9850Ga PLUS

Working With Lists

- The student must enclose the first list in ( ) and use "×" symbol to multiply.

- If the calculator will not move to highlight a list, press $\boxed{\text{EXIT}}$ to return to the menu and re-enter list. You may need to repeat this.

- You can enter a maximum of six lists in this calculator.

Regression values

- Explain what r and r^2 mean.

For the TI-83

Working With Lists

- You can change each list name from **L1, L2,** and so on, to a specific name, but first press $\boxed{\text{STAT}}$ **5:SetUpEditor** $\boxed{\text{ENTER}}$.

- To give a list a name, press $\boxed{\text{STAT}}$ **1:Edit** and highlight **L1**. Press $\boxed{\text{DEL}}$. Continue to press $\boxed{\text{DEL}}$ to remove the **L2, L3, L4, L5,** and **L6** columns. The calculator moves to the next list and prompts you to name it at the bottom of the screen. To name the list "SIDES", press $\boxed{\text{2nd}}$ $\boxed{\text{ALPHA}}$ **[A-LOCK]** $\boxed{\text{LN}}$ **[S]** $\boxed{x^2}$ **[I]** $\boxed{x^{-1}}$ **[D]** $\boxed{\text{sin}}$ **[E]** $\boxed{\text{LN}}$ **[S]** $\boxed{\text{ENTER}}$.

Regression values

- By default, the correlation coefficient **r** and the coefficient of determination **r²** are not displayed. You can display the **r** and the **r²** by pressing $\boxed{\text{2nd}}$ **O [CATALOG]**. Move the cursor down until the cursor points to **DiagnosticOn** and press $\boxed{\text{ENTER}}$ $\boxed{\text{ENTER}}$. The Home Screen will display **Done.** The calculator will now display **r** and **r²** with regression data.

       Algebra 1 Graphing Calculator Activities

Graphing Calculator Activity 4 (continued)
TEACHING SUGGESTIONS

Notes for the Activity 4

Part A The sum of the measures of the interior angles of any triangle is 180.

Part B The last page of the Teaching Suggestions contains Regular Polygons master for use in this part of Activity 4.

The following shows the completed table from the second step in Part B.

Number of sides of a regular polygon	3	4	5	6	8	10	12	n
Diagonals from one vertex	0	1	2	3	5	7	9	$n - 3$
Number of triangles formed	1	2	3	4	6	8	10	$n - 2$
Number of triangles × 180°	180°	360°	540°	720°	1080°	1440°	1800°	$(n - 2)180°$

Part C The constant rate of change is 1. The screens below show the scatterplots of the data. The completed equation is $y = 1x + (-2)$.

CASIO CFX-9850Ga PLUS   **TI-83**

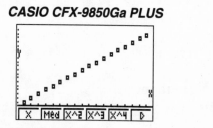   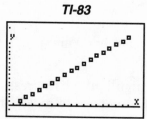

Part D Students complete the following chart.

List 1: number of sides	3	4	5	6	7	8	9	10	15	20
List 3: sum of the measures of the interior angles	180°	360°	540°	720°	900°	1080°	1260°	1440°	2340°	3240°

The constant rate of change is 180. The screens below show the scatter plots of the data. The completed equation is $y = 180x + (-360)$. As students analyze the slope and the constant rate of change, they should discover that a and the slope are both 1.

CASIO CFX-9850Ga PLUS   **TI-83**

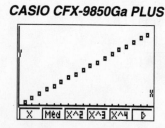   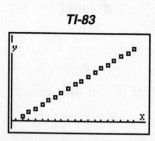

Part E Students complete the following chart relating lists 1, 4, and 5.

List 1: number of sides	3	4	6	8	10	15	20
List 4: measure of interior angle	60	90	120	135	144	156	162
List 5: measure of exterior angle	120	90	60	45	36	24	18

The sum of the measures of an interior angle and an exterior angle is 180. An interior angle and an exterior angle form a straight angle.

The sum of the measures of an interior angle and an exterior angle is 180. An interior angle and an exterior angle form a straight angle.

Graphing Calculator Activity 4 (continued)
TEACHING SUGGESTIONS

Students complete the following chart relating lists 1 and 6.

List 1: number of sides	3	4	5	6	7	8	9	10	11	12
List 6: ratio between the measures of interior and exterior angles	0.5	1	1.5	2	2.5	3	3.5	4	4.5	5

The constant rate of change is 0.5. The screens below show the scatter plots of the data. The completed equation is $y = 0.5x + (-1)$. The value a is the rate of change.

CASIO CFX-9850Ga PLUS

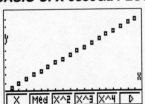

TI-83

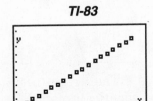

Summary

Students complete a chart describing what each list represents. The following are sample descriptions.

List 1: n; the number of sides of a polygon

List 2: $(n - 2)$; the number of triangles formed in each polygon

List 3: $(n - 2) \times 180$; the sum of the measures of the interior angles of a polygon

List 4: $\frac{(n - 2) \times 180}{n}$; the measure of each interior angle of a regular polygon

List 5: $\frac{360}{n}$; the measure of each exterior angle of a regular polygon

List 6: $\frac{n - 2}{2}$; the ratio between the measure of an interior angle and the measure of an exterior angle of a regular polygon

Students complete statements about what they have learned.

1. 180 **2.** 2 **3.** 180 **4.** the number of sides **5.** 360 **6.** the number of sides

Answers for Student Worksheet Practice

1. The rate of change is 1.

2. $y = x + 6$

3. The rate of change is 3.

4. $y = 3x - 12$

5. The rate of change is 4.

6. $y = 0.4x + 0.2$

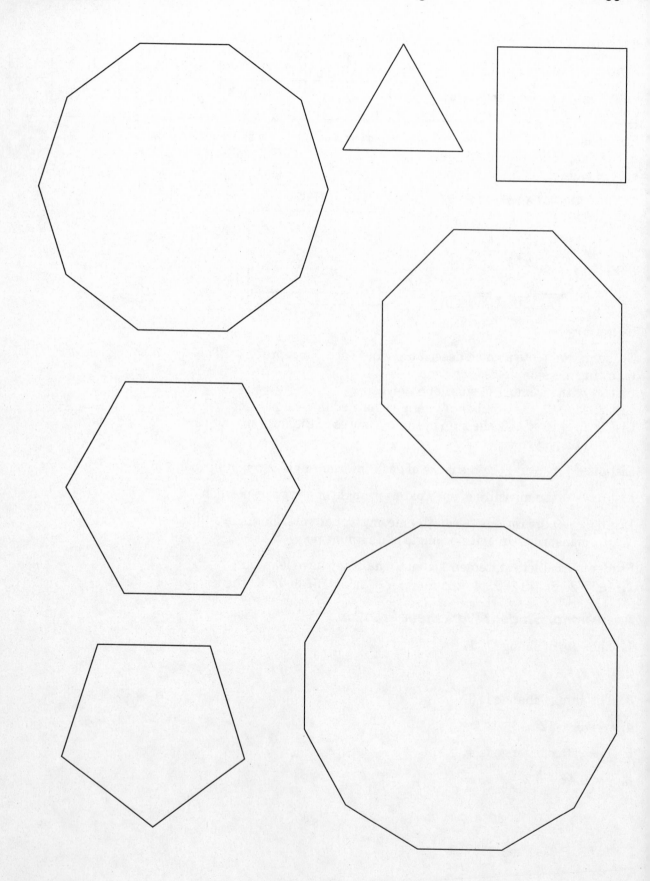

Graphing Calculator Activity 4

Recognizing Patterns:
Investigating Algebraic Relationships in Regular Polygons

You can use the graphing calculator to investigate patterns. In this activity, you will investigate polygons and use the graphing calculator to determine relationships.

Part A   Determine the sum of the measures of the interior angles of a triangle.

• Draw any triangle and label the angles 1, 2, and 3.

• Tear off the vertices of the angle.

• Place the angles adjacent to each other. The three angles will form a straight angle.

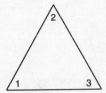 

$$m\angle 1 + m\angle 2 + m\angle 3 = 180°$$

• Repeat this experiment using triangles of different sizes and shapes. What conclusion can you draw from your experiment?

Part B   Determine the formula for the sum of the measures of the interior angles of regular polygons.

• A diagonal is a line segment joining any two non-adjacent vertices of a polygon.

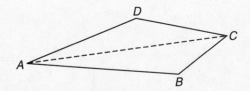

• Using the worksheet containing a triangle, a quadrilateral, a pentagon, a hexagon, an octagon, a decagon, and a dodecagon, complete the following chart.

Number of sides of a regular polygon	3	4	5	6	8	10	12	n
Diagonals from one vertex								
Number of triangles formed								$n-2$
Number of triangles × 180°								$(n-2)180°$

Part C *Explore the relationship between the number of sides of a regular polygon and the number of triangles formed.*

- In the **MAIN MENU**, press **4 [LIST]**. To clear existing lists, highlight the list heading, such as **List 1**, and press [F4] **[DEL-A]** [F1] **[YES]**. Continue until all lists are cleared. Place the cursor in the first position of the **List 1** column.

- List 1 is the number of sides of each regular polygon. You can enter the data in the calculator manually.

  Enter: 3 [EXE] **4** [EXE] **5** [EXE] **... 20** [EXE]

  Or, you can use the sequence feature to complete the list. First, highlight **List 1**. Then, use the following commands to list the numbers from 3 to 20 by increments of 1.

  Enter: [OPTN] [F1] **[LIST]** [F5] **[Seq]** [X,θ,T] [,] [X,θ,T] [,] **3** [,]
  20 [,] **1** [)] [EXE]

- List 2 is the number of triangles formed in each regular polygon. You can enter the data in the calculator manually.

  Enter: 1 [EXE] **2** [EXE] **3** [EXE] **... 18** [EXE]

  Or, you can use the calculator to calculate the values. Recall that the number of triangles formed in a regular polygon is $n - 2$, where n is the number of sides of the polygon. Highlight **List 2** and use the following commands.

  Enter: [F1] **[List] 1** [−] **2** [EXE]

- Examine the pattern.

List 1: number of sides of a regular polygon (n)	3	4	5	6	7	8	9	10	15	20
List 2: number of triangles formed ($n - 2$)	1	2	3	4	5	6	7	8	13	18

The rate of change is determined by the ratio $\frac{\Delta \text{List 2}}{\Delta \text{List 1}}$. You can use the Δ feature to find the rate of change. Highlight **List 3** and use the following commands.

Enter: MENU 1 [RUN] OPTN F1 [LIST] F6 [▷] F6 [▷] F5
[△] 2 ÷ F5 [△] 1

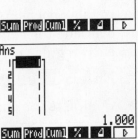

Now, press EXE.
What is the constant rate of change? _____

• Explore the functional relationship using the graphing calculator.

Enter: MENU 2 [STAT]   Your list will appear in the **STAT MODE**.

F1 [GRPH] F6 [SET]   Set up a scatter plot to compare List 1 and List 2.

Highlight each category and
use the soft function keys to
select your options. Then press
EXIT F4 [SEL].

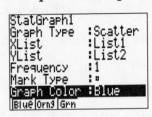

Press F1 [On] to turn on **StatGraph1**. Be sure other **StatGraphs** are off.
Then press F6 [DRAW].

Sketch the scatter plot. Label the axes.

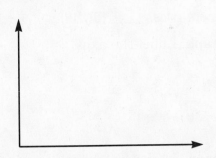

• Determine the line of best fit and examine the slope (rate of change).

Enter: F1 [X]

The screen display is shown at the right.

Complete the statement $y =$ _____ $x +$ _____.

The x coefficient, a, is the rate of change. Does this match the
rate of change you found earlier? _____

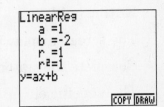

• Draw the line of best fit on the calculator.

Enter: F5 [COPY] EXE   to store the new equation
F6 [DRAW]   to draw the line of best fit

Part D *Explore the functional relationship between the number of sides of a regular polygon and the sum of the measures of its interior angles.*

- List 3 is the sum of the measures of the interior angles of each regular polygon. First press MENU 4 [LIST]. Then highlight **List 3** to override the existing data in **List 3**. The sum of the interior angles of each regular polygon equals $(n - 2) \times 180$.

  Enter: OPTN F1 [LIST] F1 [List] 2 × 180 EXE

- Complete the chart.

List 1: number of sides of a regular polygon (*n*)	3	4	5	6	7	8	9	10	15	20
List 3: sum of the measures of the interior angles ((*n* − 2) × 180)	180°									3,240°

- The rate of change is determined by the ratio $\frac{\Delta \text{List } 3}{\Delta \text{List } 1}$. Follow the method you used to find $\frac{\Delta \text{List } 2}{\Delta \text{List } 1}$. Be sure to highlight **List 4**.

  What is the constant rate of change for this relation?

- Explore the functional relationship using the graphing calculator.

  Enter: MENU 2 [STAT] F1 [GRPH] F6 [SET]

  Change the **Ylist** to List 3 by highlighting **Ylist** and pressing F3 [List3] EXIT . Then press F4 [SEL].

  If **StatGraph1** is on, press F6 [DRAW].

  Sketch the graph. Label the axes.

- Determine the line of best fit and examine the slope (rate of change).

  Enter: F1 [X]

  The screen display is shown at the right.

  Complete the statement $y = $ _____ $x + $ _____.

  The *x* coefficient, *a*, is the rate of change (slope). Do you agree with this value?

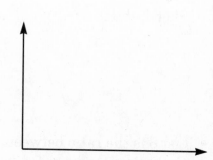

- Draw the line of best fit on the calculator.

Enter: [F5] [COPY] [EXE]   to store the new equation
          [F6] [DRAW]   to draw the line of best fit

Part E   Explore the relationship between the interior and exterior angles of regular polygons.

- List 4 is the measure of each interior angle of each regular polygon. To find the measure of each interior angle, divide the sum of the interior angles (List 3) by the number of sides in each polygon (List 1). Press [MENU] 4 [LIST], and move the cursor to highlight **List 4**.

Enter: [OPTN] [F1] [LIST] [F1] [List] 3 [÷] [F1] [List] 1 [EXE]

- List 5 is the measure of each exterior angle of each regular polygon. The sum of the exterior angles of any regular polygon is 360°. To find the degree measure of each exterior angle of a regular polygon, divide 360 by the number of sides in the polygon. Highlight **List 5**.

Enter: 360 [÷] [F1] [List] 1 [EXE]

- Complete the chart.

List 1: number of sides of a regular polygon (n)	3	4	6	8	10	15	20
List 4: measure of interior angle	60						162
List 5: measure of exterior angle (360 ÷ n)	120						18

What is the sum of the measures of an interior angle and an exterior angle of a regular polygon? Why?

- List 6 is the ratio between the measure of an interior angle and the measure of an exterior angle of each regular polygon. Highlight **List 6**.

Enter: [OPTN] [F1] [LIST] [F1] [List] 4 [÷] [F1] [List] 5 [EXE]

- Complete the chart.

List 1: number of sides of a regular polygon	3	4	5	6	7	8	9	10	11	12
List 6: ratio between the measures of interior and exterior angles	0.5									5

- The rate of change is determined by the ratio $\frac{\Delta \text{List } 6}{\Delta \text{List } 1}$. Return to the **RUN MODE** by pressing MENU **1 [RUN]**.

  Enter: OPTN F1 **[LIST]** F6 [▷] F6 [▷] F5 [△] **6** ÷ F5 [△] **1** EXE

  What is the constant rate of change for this relation?

- Explore the functional relationship using the graphing calculator.

  Enter: MENU **2 [STAT]** F1 **[GRPH]** F6 **[SET]**

  Set up a scatterplot to compare List 1 and List 6. Change the **Ylist** to List 6 by highlighting **Ylist** and pressing F6 **[List6]** EXIT . Then press F4 **[SEL]**.

  If **StatGraph1** is on, press F6 **[DRAW]**. Be sure other **StatGraphs** are off.

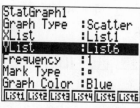

  Sketch the graph. Label the axes.

- Determine the line of best fit and examine the slope (rate of change).

  Enter: F1 **[X]**

  The screen display is shown at the right.

  Complete the statement $y = $ _____ $x + $ _____.

  The x coefficient, a, is the rate of change. Do you agree?

- Draw the line of best fit on the calculator.

  Enter: F5 **[COPY]** EXE   to store the new equation
  F6 **[DRAW]**   to draw the line

Summary

Check for Understanding

Describe in words the contents of each list and explain what the data represents.

List 1	List 2	List 3	List 4	List 5	List 6

Complete each statement.

1. The sum of the measures of the interior angles of a triangle is

   _____.

2. The number of triangles formed in a polygon can be represented by

   the formula $n -$ _____.

3. The sum of the measures of the interior angles of a regular polygon

   is determined by the formula $(n - 2) \times$ _____.

4. To determine the measure of each interior angle of a regular
   polygon, divide the sum of the measures of the interior angles by

   _____.

5. The sum of the measures of the exterior angles of a polygon is

   always _____.

6. To determine the measure of each exterior angle of a regular

   polygon, divide 360 by _____.

Graphing Calculator Activity 4

Recognizing Patterns:
Investigating Algebraic Relationships in Regular Polygons

You can use the graphing calculator to investigate patterns. In this activity, you will investigate polygons and use the graphing calculator to determine relationships.

Part A   Determine the sum of the measures of the interior angles of a triangle.

- Draw any triangle and label the angles 1, 2, and 3.

- Tear off the vertices of the angle.

- Place the angles adjacent to each other. The three angles will form a straight angle.

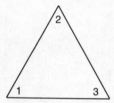 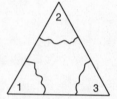

$$m\angle 1 + m\angle 2 + m\angle 3 = 180°$$

- Repeat this experiment using triangles of different sizes and shapes. What conclusion can you draw from your experiment?

Part B   Determine the formula for the sum of the measures of the interior angles of regular polygons.

- A diagonal is a line segment joining any two non-adjacent vertices of a polygon.

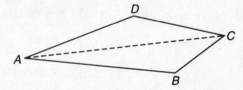

- Using the worksheet containing a triangle, a quadrilateral, a pentagon, a hexagon, an octagon, a decagon, and a dodecagon, complete the following chart.

Number of sides of a regular polygon	3	4	5	6	8	10	12	n
Diagonals from one vertex								
Number of triangles formed								$n-2$
Number of triangles × 180°								$(n-2)180°$

NAME _____ DATE _____

Graphing Calculator Activity 4 (continued)   TI-83 Keystrokes

Part C Explore the relationship between the number of sides of a regular polygon and the number of triangles formed.

- Press [STAT], select **1:Edit...**, and clear existing lists. To clear existing lists, move cursor up to highlight **L1**. Press [CLEAR] [ENTER]. Highlight **L2**. Press [CLEAR] [ENTER]. Continue until all lists are cleared. Place cursor in the first position of the **L1** column.

- List 1 is the number of sides of each regular polygon. You can enter the data in the calculator manually.

  Enter: 3 [ENTER] **4** [ENTER] **5** [ENTER] ... **20** [ENTER]

  Or, you can use the sequence feature to complete the list. First, highlight **L1**. Then, use the following commands to list the numbers from 3 to 20 by increments of 1.

  Enter: [2nd] [STAT] **[LIST]** [▶] (to highlight **OPS**) **5** (to select **seq**)
  [X,T,θ,n] [,] [X,T,θ,n] [,] **3** [,] **20** [,] **1** [)] [ENTER]

- List 2 is the number of triangles formed in each regular polygon. You can enter the data in the calculator manually.

  Enter: 1 [ENTER] **2** [ENTER] **3** [ENTER] ... **18** [ENTER]

  Or, you can use the calculator to calculate the values. Recall that the number of triangles formed in a regular polygon is $n - 2$ where n is the number of sides of the polygon. Highlight **L2** and use the following commands.

  Enter: [2nd] **1** [L1] [−] **2** [ENTER]

- Examine the pattern.

List 1: number of sides of a regular polygon (n)	3	4	5	6	7	8	9	10	15	20
List 2: number of triangles formed ($n - 2$)	1	2	3	4	5	6	7	8	13	18

The rate of change is determined by the ratio $\frac{\Delta \text{LIST } 2}{\Delta \text{LIST } 1}$. You can use the Δ feature to find the rate of change. Highlight **L3** and use the following commands.

  Enter: [2nd] [STAT] **[LIST]** [▶] (to highlight **OPS**) **7** (to select **List**)
  [2nd] **2** [L2] [)] [÷] [2nd] [STAT] **[LIST]** [▶] (to highlight **OPS**) **7**
  (to select **ΔList**) [2nd] **1** [L1] [)] [ENTER]

What is the constant rate of change?

© Glencoe/McGraw-Hill   **49**   *Algebra 1 Graphing Calculator Activities*

- Explore the functional relationship using the graphing calculator. Press Y=. If there are existing equations, clear them by pressing CLEAR.

  Enter: 2nd Y= [STAT PLOT]

  You want **Plot 1** turned on and the others turned off. Select **1:Plot1.** Highlight your selection and press ENTER.

  To set the **Xlist**, press 2nd 1 [L1].

  To set the **Ylist**, press 2nd 2 [L2].

  Press ZOOM, move the cursor down to **9:ZoomStat**, and press ENTER.

  Sketch the scatter plot. Label the axes.

- Determine the line of best fit and examine the slope (rate of change).

  Enter: STAT ▶ (to highlight **CALC**) 4 (to select
       LinReg(ax+b)) 2nd 1 [LI] , 2nd 2 [L2] ENTER

  The screen display is shown at the right.

  Complete the statement $y =$ _____ $x +$ _____.

  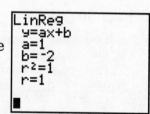

  The x coefficient, a, is the rate of change. Does this match the rate of change you found earlier?

- Draw the line of best fit on the calculator.

  Enter: Y= VARS 5 (to select **Statistics ...**) ▶ ▶ (to highlight **EQ**)
       1 (to select **RegEQ**) GRAPH

Part D   *Explore the functional relationship between the number of sides of a regular polygon and the sum of the measures of its interior angles.*

- List 3 is the sum of the measures of the interior angles of each regular polygon. First press STAT, and select **1:Edit**. Then highlight **L3** to override the existing data in List 3. The sum of the interior angles of each regular polygon equals $(n - 2) \times 180$.

  Enter: 2nd 2 [L2] × 180 ENTER

- Complete the chart.

List 1: number of sides of a regular polygon (n)	3	4	5	6	7	8	9	10	15	20
List 3: sum of the measures of the interior angles (($n - 2$) × 180)	180°									3,240°

- The rate of change is determined by the ratio $\frac{\Delta \text{List 3}}{\Delta \text{List 1}}$. Follow the method to find $\frac{\Delta \text{List 2}}{\Delta \text{List 1}}$. Be sure to highlight **List 4**. What is the constant rate of change for this relation?

- Explore the functional relationship using the graphing calculator. Press Y= and clear all existing equations using CLEAR.

Enter: 2nd Y= [STAT PLOT]

You want **Plot 1** turned on and all others turned off. Select **1:Plot1**. Highlight your selection and press ENTER.

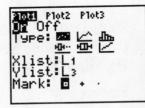

To set the **Xlist**, press 2nd **1 [L1]**.

To set the **Ylist**, press 2nd **3 [L3]**.

Press ZOOM, move the cursor down to **9:ZoomStat**, and press ENTER.

Sketch the graph. Label the axes.

- Determine the line of best fit and examine the slope (rate of change).

Enter: STAT ▶ (to highlight **CALC**) **4** (to select **LinReg(ax+b)**) 2nd
   1 [L1] , 2nd **3 [L3]** ENTER

The screen display is shown at the right.

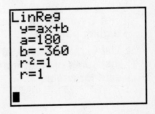

Complete the statement $y =$ _____ $x +$ _____.

- Draw the line of best fit on the calculator.

  Enter: Y= VARS **5** (to select **Statistics...**) ▶ ▶ (to highlight **EQ**)
  1 (to select **RegEQ**) GRAPH

Part E *Explore the relationship between the interior and exterior angles of regular polygons.*

- List 4 is the measure of each interior angle of each regular polygon. To find the measure of each interior angle, divide the sum of the interior angles (List 3) by the number of sides in each polygon (List 1). Press STAT , select **1:Edit**, and move the cursor to highlight **L4**.

  Enter: 2nd **3** [L3] ÷ 2nd **1** [L1] ENTER

- List 5 is the measure of each exterior angle of each regular polygon. The sum of the exterior angles of any regular polygon is 360°. To find the degree measure of each exterior angle of a regular polygon, divide 360 by the number of sides in the polygon. Highlight **L5**.

  Enter: 360 ÷ **1** [LI] ENTER

- Complete the chart.

List 1: number of sides of a regular polygon (*n*)	3	4	6	8	10	15	20
List 4: measure of interior angle	60						162
List 5: measure of exterior angle (360 ÷ *n*)	120						18

What is the sum of the measures of an interior angle and an exterior angle of a regular polygon? Why?

- List 6 is the ratio between the measure of an interior angle and the measure of an exterior angle of each regular polygon. Highlight **L6**.

  Enter: 2nd **4** [L4] ÷ 2nd **5** [L5] ENTER

- Complete the chart.

List 1: number of sides of a regular polygon	3	4	5	6	7	8	9	10	11	12
List 6: ratio between the measures of interior and exterior angles	0.5									5

- The rate of change is determined by the ratio $\frac{\Delta \text{List } 6}{\Delta \text{List } 1}$. Return to

  the **Home Screen** by pressing 2nd MODE [QUIT].

  Enter: 2nd STAT [LIST] ▶ (to highlight OPS) 7 (to select ↓ΔList)
  2nd 6 [L6]) ÷ 2nd STAT [LIST] ▶ (to highlight OPS) 7
  (to select ↓ΔList) 2nd 1 [L1]) ENTER

  What is the constant rate of change for this relation?

- Explore the functional relationship using the graphing calculator. Press Y= , and clear all equations using CLEAR .

  Enter: 2nd Y= [STAT PLOT]

  You want **Plot 1** turned on and all others turned off. Select **1:Plot1**.

  To set the **Xlist**, press 2nd 1 [L1].

  To set the **Ylist**, press 2nd 6 [L6].

  Press ZOOM , move cursor to **9:ZoomStat**, and press ENTER .

  Sketch the graph. Label the axes.

  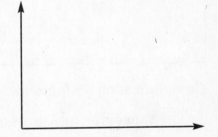

- Determine the line of best fit and examine the slope (rate of change).

  Enter: STAT ▶ (to highlight CALC) 4 (to select
  LinReg(ax+b)) 2nd 1 [L1] , 2nd 6 [L6] ENTER

  The screen display is shown at the right.

  Complete the statement $y = $ _____ $x + $ _____.

  The x coefficient, a, is the rate of change. Do you agree?

  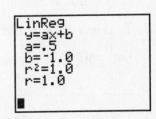

- Draw the line of best fit on the calculator.

  Enter: Y= VARS 5 (to select Statistics…) ▶ ▶ (to highlight EQ) 1
  (to select RegEQ) GRAPH

Summary

Check for Understanding

Describe in words the contents of each list and explain what the data represents.

List 1	List 2	List 3	List 4	List 5	List 6

Complete each statement.

1. The sum of the measures of the interior angles of a triangle is

   _____.

2. The number of triangles formed in a polygon can be represented by

   the formula $n -$ _____.

3. The sum of the measures of the interior angles of a regular

   polygon is determined by the formula $(n - 2) \times$ _____.

4. To determine the measure of each interior angle of a regular

   polygon, divide the sum of the measures of the interior angles by

   _____.

5. The sum of the measures of the exterior angles of a polygon is

   always _____.

6. To determine the measure of each exterior angle of a regular

   polygon, divide 360 by _____.

Graphing Calculator Activity 4

Recognizing Patterns:
Investigating Algebraic Relationships in Regular Polygons

Practice

Study each table and answer each question.

List 1	1	2	3	4	5	6	7	8	9	10
List 2	7	8	9	10	11	12	13	14	15	16

1. Determine the rate of change.

2. Determine the equation of the line of best fit using the graphing calculator.

List 1	5	6	7	8	9	10	11	12	13	14	15
List 2	3	6	9	12	15	18	21	24	27	30	33

3. Determine the rate of change.

4. Determine the equation of the line of best fit using the graphing calculator.

List 1	2	3	4	5	6	7	8	9
List 2	1	1.4	1.8	2.2	2.6	3	3.4	3.8

5. Determine the rate of change.

6. Determine the equation of the line of best fit using the graphing calculator.

Graphing Calculator Activity 5

TEACHING SUGGESTIONS

Analyzing Linear Equations

Objective   The student will write an equation of a line when given the graph of the line, two points on the line, or the slope and a point on the line.

Use with GLENCOE Algebra 1: Integration, Applications, and Connections		
Lesson	Lesson Title	Student Edition Pages
6-2	Writing Linear Equations in Point-Slope and Standard Form and Standard Form	332-338

Hints

- Each calculator has particular protocols with certain procedures. You may find it helpful to practice each lesson before teaching it.

For the CASIO CFX-9850Ga PLUS

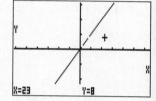

- This activity allows students to generate the equation of the line that goes through two specified points, graph using the calculator; and test to see if the two points are truly on that line.

- The procedure tests the accuracy of the equation by *UNPLOTTING* the two points that are given. If there are no "holes" in the graph after the points are unplotted, then the equation that the students found is incorrect, and they should rework the equation.

- Enclose all fractions within parentheses.

For the TI-83

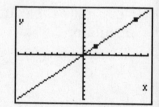

- This activity allows students to generate the equation of the line that goes through two specified points, graph using the calculator, and test to see if the two points are truly on that line.

- The procedure tests the accuracy of the equation by *HIGHLIGHTING* the two points that are given. If the highlighted points are not on the graph, then the equation that the students found is incorrect and they should rework the equation.

Answers for Student Worksheet Practice

1. D

2. A

3. C

4. B

Graphing Calculator Activity 5

Analyzing Linear Equations

You can use the graphing calculator to determine if points are located on the graph of a function.

Write the slope-intercept form of the equation of the line that passes through (2, 2) and (8, 8). Use the graphing calculator to verify your equation.

- From the **MAIN MENU**, press **5 [GRAPH]**. Clear out existing equations by highlighting each equation, and pressing F2 **[DEL]** F1 **[YES]**.

- The top of the window should display **Graph Func:Y=**. If not, press F3 **[TYPE]** F1 **[Y=]**.

- To set the standard $[-10, 10]$ by $[-10, 10]$ window, press SHIFT F3 **[V-WIN]** F3 **[STD]** EXIT .

- Determine the slope-intercept form of the equation of the line that passes through (2, 2) and (8, 8).

- Since the equation is $y = x$, enter the equation by highlighting **Y1:** and then pressing X,θ,T EXE F6 **[DRAW]**.

- To view the graph on an integer scale, press SHIFT F2 **[ZOOM]** F6 **[▷]** F4 **[INTG]**.

- To clear out existing points saved in the draw function, press SHIFT F4 **[SKTCH]** F1 **[C1s]**.

- Now highlight the two points on the graph to determine if the points are on the line.

  Enter: SHIFT F4 **[SKTCH]** F6 **[▷]** F1 **[PLOT]** F3 **[P1-Off]**

- Move the cursor until **X = 2** and **Y = 2** is displayed at the bottom of the screen. Press EXE .

- Locate the point (8, 8) and press EXE .

  Use the arrow keys to move the cursor away from the line. The line graph now has holes at (2, 2) and (8, 8), showing that the line does contain the two points.

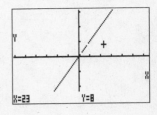

Analyzing Linear Equations

Practice

Write the slope-intercept form of the equation of the line that passes through each pair of points. Use the graphing calculator to verify your equation. Select the correct graphic image.

1. $(-1, 2), (3, 7)$

$y =$ _____

A.

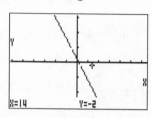

2. $(-5, 9), (3, -2)$

$y =$ _____

B.

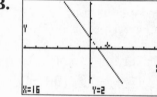

3. $(6, -2), (20, 8)$

$y =$ _____

C.

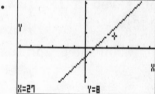

4. $(2, 5), (5, 2)$

$y =$ _____

D.

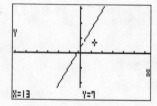

Graphing Calculator Activity 5

TI-83 Keystrokes

Analyzing Linear Equations

You can use the graphing calculator to determine if points are located on the graph of a function.

Write the slope-intercept form of the equation of the line that passes through (2, 2) and (8, 8). Use the graphing calculator to verify your equation.

- From the **Home Screen**, press $\boxed{Y=}$. Highlight each existing equation, and press $\boxed{CLEAR}$.

- To set the standard $[-10, 10]$ by $[-10, 10]$ window, press $\boxed{ZOOM}$ and select **6:Zstandard**.

- Delete existing points and pictures previously stored.

  Enter: $\boxed{2nd}$ $\boxed{MODE}$ [QUIT] $\boxed{2nd}$ $\boxed{PRGM}$ [DRAW] 1 (to select **ClrDraw**)
  $\boxed{ENTER}$

- Determine the slope-intercept form of the equation of the line that passes through (2, 2) and (8, 8).

- Since the equation is $y = x$, enter the equation by pressing $\boxed{Y=}$ $\boxed{X,T,\theta,n}$ $\boxed{GRAPH}$.

- To view the graph on an integer scale, press $\boxed{ZOOM}$ and select **8:Zinteger** $\boxed{ENTER}$.

- You will now plot the two points on the graph to determine if the points are on the line.

  Enter: $\boxed{2nd}$ $\boxed{MODE}$ [QUIT] $\boxed{2nd}$ $\boxed{PRGM}$ [DRAW] $\boxed{\blacktriangleright}$ (to highlight
  POINTS) 1 (to select **Pt-On**) 2 $\boxed{,}$ 2 $\boxed{,}$ 2 $\boxed{)}$ $\boxed{ALPHA}$ $\boxed{.}$ [:]
  $\boxed{2nd}$ $\boxed{PRGM}$ [DRAW] $\boxed{\blacktriangleright}$ (to highlight **POINTS**) 1 (to select
  Pt-On) 8 $\boxed{,}$ 8 $\boxed{,}$ 2 $\boxed{)}$

  Your **Home Screen** will read **Pt-On(2,2,2):Pt-On(8,8,2)**. **Pt-On(2,2,2)** is the format for (*x, y,* type of marker). You may choose the type of marker. 1 shows a solid dot, 2 shows an open or solid box, and 3 shows a cross.

  If you press $\boxed{ENTER}$ the line graph appears with both points on the line.

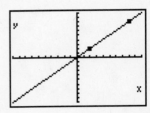

Graphing Calculator Activity 5

Analyzing Linear Equations

Practice

Write the slope-intercept form of the equation of the line that passes through each pair of points. Use the graphing calculator to verify your equation. Select the correct graphic image.

1. $(-1, 2), (3, 7)$

   $y =$ _____

A.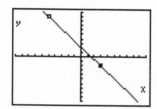

2. $(-5, 9), (3, -2)$

   $y =$ _____

B.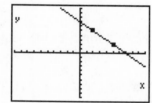

3. $(6, -2), (20, 8)$

   $y =$ _____

C.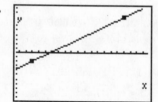

4. $(2, 5), (5, 2)$

   $y =$ _____

D.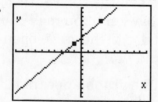

Graphing Calculator Activity 6

TEACHING SUGGESTIONS

Solving Systems of Linear Equations

Objective   The student will solve systems of two linear equations in two variables, both algebraically and graphically and apply these techniques to solve practical problems. Graphing calculators will be used as both a primary tool of solutions and to confirm an algebraic solution.

Use with GLENCOE Algebra 1: Integration, Applications, and Connections

Lesson	Lesson Title	Student Edition Pages
8-1	Graphing Systems of Equations	454-461
8-2	Substitution	462-468
8-3	Elimination Using Addition and Subtraction	469-473
8-4	Elimination Using Multiplication	475-481

Hints

- Each calculator has particular protocols with certain procedures. You may find it helpful to practice each lesson before teaching it.

For the CASIO CFX-9850Ga PLUS

- From the **MAIN MENU**, select **5 [GRAPH]**.
- Highlight any existing equations and use a F2 **[DEL]** and F1 **[YES]** to clear out the unwanted equations.
- Select the standard viewing window [−10, 10] by [−10, 10] by pressing SHIFT F3 **[V-Window]** F3 **[STD]**. Pressing EXIT returns the calculator to **GRAPH Mode.**

NOTE: In **GRAPH Mode**, selecting F3 **[TYPE]** allows a choice of equalities: Press F1 to select **Y=** or press F4 to select **X=C**. To access the inequalities, press F6 [▷] and choose F1 , F2 , F3 , or F4 to select the desired inequality.

- The student page includes instructions for entering each equation of the system and how to apply color to each graph.
- Students use the **TRACE** function to explore and approximate the intersection point of the two graphs. The right and left arrow keys move the cursor along the graph and the up and down arrow keys toggle the cursor between the two graphs.

NOTE: There are special functions that pinpoint commonly desired values more exactly. To access this menu, press SHIFT F5 **[G-Solv]**. Then select the value you wish to find.

- To find the x-intercept, select F1 **[ROOT]**.
- To find the y-intercept, select F4 **[Y-ICPT]**.
- To find the intersection point of two graphs, select F5 **[ISCT]**.
- To find a particular y value for a specific x value with the coordinates of this point displayed on the graph, select F6 [▷] and then F1 **[Y-CAL]**. Selecting F2 **[X-CAL]** finds an x value for a given y value.

For the TI-83

- From the **Home Screen**, press ⌈Y=⌉. Highlight any existing equations using the up or down arrow keys and press ⌈CLEAR⌉.

- To select the standard viewing window, press ⌈ZOOM⌉ and select **6:Zstandard.**

- Make sure all statistical graphs are turned off by pressing ⌈2nd⌉ ⌈Y=⌉ [STAT PLOT] and selecting **4:PlotsOff.**

- For the proper setup, have students press ⌈MODE⌉ and match your settings to the first screen shown below. Then press ⌈2nd⌉ ⌈ZOOM⌉ [FORMAT] and match your settings to the second screen.

- The student page includes instructions for entering each equation of the system.

- Students use ⌈TRACE⌉ and the arrow keys to explore and approximate the intersection point of the two graphs. The right and left arrow keys move the cursor along the graph and the up and down arrow keys toggle the cursor between the two graphs.

NOTE: There are special functions that pinpoint commonly desired values more exactly. To access this menu, press ⌈2nd⌉ ⌈TRACE⌉ [CALC]. Then select the value you wish to find.

- To find the *y* value for a given *x* value, select **1:value.** Use the up or down arrows to find the *y* value for more than one function at a particular *x* value.

- To find the zero (*x*-intercept or root) of an equation, select **2:zero.** See the TI-83 Graphing Calculator Guidebook, Section 3-26 Function Graphing for detailed instructions.

- To find the point of intersection between two graphs, select **5:intersect.** The calculator will prompt you to select which two curves you want to use. Use the up or down arrow keys to identify the first curve (equation) then press ⌈ENTER⌉. The screen asks **Second curve?** Move the cursor to the second equation then press ⌈ENTER⌉. The screen now asks **Guess?** Move the cursor, using the right/left arrow keys, to the approximate point of intersection and press ⌈ENTER⌉. The cursor is now on the point of intersection and the coordinates are shown.

Answers for Student Worksheet Practice

1. $(2, 5)$ **2.** $(9, 1)$ **3.** $(-4, 3)$ **4.** $(5, -1)$ **5.** $(7, 2)$ **6.** $(6, 7)$

Graphing Calculator Activity 6

Solving Systems of Linear Equations

You can use the graphing calculator to solve a system of linear equations graphically or algebraically.

Graph the system of equations and find the solution (point of intersection).

$$-2x + y = -4$$
$$2x + y = -4$$

- From the **MAIN MENU**, press **5 [GRAPH]**. Clear out existing equations by highlighting them and pressing F2 **[DEL]** F1 **[YES]**.

- Set the View Window by pressing SHIFT F3 **[V-WIN]** F3 **[STD]** EXIT .

- The top of the window should display **Graph Func:Y=**. If not, press F3 **[TYPE]** F1 **[Y=]**.

- Solve the first equation for *y*. Enter the equation ($y = 2x - 4$) in the **Y1** position.
  Enter: 2 X,θ,T — 4 EXE

- Solve the second equation for *y*. Enter the equation ($y = -2x - 4$) in the **Y2** position.
  Enter: (−) **2** X,θ,T — 4 EXE

- Highlight **Y1=** and press F4 **[COLR]** F2 **[Orng]**. Highlight **Y2=** and press F3 **[Grn]** EXIT . Then press F6 **[DRAW]**. The graph of the two equations appears on the screen.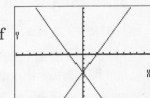

- To find the point of intersection, press SHIFT F1 **[TRCE]** and use the right/left arrow keys to approximate the intersection point. To check for integer solutions, press SHIFT F2 **[ZOOM]** F6 **[▷]** F4 **[INTG]**. The graph is redrawn using a new scale. Press SHIFT F1 **[TRCE]** , and use the right/left arrow keys to locate the apparent point of intersection. Use the up/down keys to verify that the apparent point of intersection is actually located on each line. The solution should be (0, −4).

Graphing Calculator Activity 6 (continued)

- Use the graphing calculator to check your answer. Press MENU 1 [RUN] to return to **RUN MODE**. Check to see if (0, −4) is a solution of the first equation.

  Enter: (−) 2 (0) + (−) 4 EXE

  Since the answer is −4, (0, −4) is a solution of the first equation. Now, check to see if (0, −4) is a solution of the second equation.

  Enter: 2 (0) + (−) 4 EXE

  Since the answer is −4, (0, −4) is a solution of the second equation. Therefore, (0, −4) is the common solution or point of intersection of the two equations.

Solve the system of equations algebraically using elimination.

To solve the system of equations using the graphing calculator, you will create a matrix to represent each equation. To create the matrices, each equation must be in standard form ($Ax + By = C$). Each matrix will have one row and three columns. The first column represents the coefficient of x, or A. The second column represents the coefficient of y, or B. The third column represents the constant, or C.

- Clear all existing matrices.

  Enter: MENU 3 [MAT] F2 [DEL-A] F1 [YES]

- Matrix A will represent the equation $-2x + y = -4$. Highlight **Mat A**. Define the matrix as one row and three columns.

  Enter: 1 EXE 3 EXE

  Then enter the values in the matrix.

  Enter: (−) 2 EXE 1 EXE (−) 4 EXE EXIT

- Matrix B will represent the equation $2x + y = -4$. Highlight **Mat B**. Define the matrix as one row and three columns.

  Enter: 1 EXE 3 EXE

  Then enter the values in the matrix.

  Enter: 2 EXE 1 EXE (−) 4 EXE EXIT

- To eliminate the variable y, multiply matrix A by −1 and add matrix B.

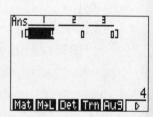

Enter: MENU 1 [RUN] OPTN F2 [MAT] (−) 1 × F1 [Mat] ALPHA
X,θ,T [A] + F1 [Mat] ALPHA log [B] EXE

Enter the equation $(4x + 0y = 0)$ from the answer matrix on the calculator.

Enter: 4 X,θ,T + 0 ALPHA − [Y] SHIFT · [=] 0 EXE

Solve this equation and store the value of x.

Enter: 0 ⟶ X,θ,T EXE

- To eliminate the variable x, add matrix A and matrix B.

Enter: OPTN F2 [MAT] F1 [Mat] ALPHA X,θ,T [A] + F1
[Mat] ALPHA log [B] EXE

Enter the equation $(0x + 2y = -8)$ from the answer matrix on the calculator.

Enter: 0 X,θ,T + 2 ALPHA − [Y] SHIFT · [=] (−) 8 EXE

Solve this equation and store the value of y.

Enter: (−) 4 ⟶ ALPHA − [Y] EXE

The solution of the system of equations is $(0, -4)$.

- Check the solution by entering each equation into the calculator.

Enter: (−) 2 X,θ,T + ALPHA − [Y] SHIFT · [=] (−) 4 EXE

The 1 indicates that $(0, -4)$ is a solution of the equation
$-2x + y = -4$.

Enter: 2 X,θ,T + ALPHA − [Y] SHIFT · [=] (−) 4 EXE

The 1 indicates that $(0, -4)$ is a solution of the equation
$2x + y = -4$. Since $(0, -4)$ is a solution to each equation, it is the solution to the system to equations.

Graphing Calculator Activity 6

Solving Systems of Linear Equations

You can use the graphing calculator to solve a system of linear
equations graphically or algebraically.

**Graph the system of equations and find the solution (point of
intersection).**

$$-2x + y = -4$$
$$2x + y = -4$$

- From the **Home Screen**, set the view window by pressing $\boxed{\text{ZOOM}}$ and
  selecting **6:Zstandard**.

- Press $\boxed{\text{Y=}}$. Highlight any existing equations using the up/down arrow
  keys and delete them by pressing $\boxed{\text{CLEAR}}$.

- Solve the first equation for y. Enter the equation ($y = 2x - 4$) in
  the **Y1** position.
  Enter: 2 $\boxed{\text{X,T,}\theta,n}$ $\boxed{-}$ 4 $\boxed{\text{ENTER}}$

- Solve the second equation for y. Enter the equation ($y = -2x - 4$)
  in the **Y2** position.
  Enter: $\boxed{\text{(-)}}$ 2 $\boxed{\text{X,T,}\theta,n}$ $\boxed{-}$ 4 $\boxed{\text{GRAPH}}$

  The graph of the two equations will appear on the screen.

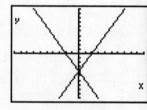

- To find the point of intersection, press $\boxed{\text{TRACE}}$ and use the
  right/left arrow keys to approximate the intersection point. To
  check for integer solutions, press $\boxed{\text{ZOOM}}$, select **8:Zinteger**, and
  press $\boxed{\text{ENTER}}$. The graph is redrawn using a new scale. Press
  $\boxed{\text{TRACE}}$, and use the right/left arrow keys to locate the apparent
  point of intersection. Use the up/down keys to verify that the
  apparent point of intersection is actually located on each line. The
  solution should be $(0, -4)$.

NOTE: You can use the arrow keys to redefine the center of the
graph. Pressing $\boxed{\text{ZOOM}}$ and selecting **8:Zinteger** takes you back to
the last graph. To view the redrawn graph, you must press $\boxed{\text{ENTER}}$.

- Use the graphing calculator to check your answer. Press
  2nd MODE [QUIT] or press CLEAR to return to the **Home Screen.**
  Check to see if (0, −4) is a solution of the first equation.

  Enter: (−) 2 (0) + (−) 4 ENTER

  Since the answer is −4, (0, −4) is a solution of the first equation.
  Now, check to see if (0, −4) is a solution of the second equation.

  Enter: 2 (0) + (−) 4 ENTER

  Since the answer is −4, (0, −4) is a solution of the second equation.
  Therefore, (0, −4) is the common solution or point of intersection of
  the two equations.

Solve the system of equations algebraically using elimination.

To solve the system of equations using the graphing calculator, you
will create a matrix to represent each equation. To create the
matrices, each equation must be in standard form $(Ax + By = C)$.
Each matrix will have one row and three columns. The first column
represents the coefficient of x, or A. The second column represents the
coefficient of y, or B. The third column represents the constant, or C.

- Clear all existing matrices.

  Enter: 2nd + [MEM] **2** (to select **Delete**) **5** (to select **Matrix**) ENTER

  Continue pressing ENTER until all matrices are deleted.

- Matrix A will represent the equation $-2x + y = -4$. Press MATRX ,
  highlight **EDIT**, and select **1:[A]**. Define the matrix as one row and
  three columns.

  Enter: 1 ENTER 3 ENTER

  Then enter the values in the matrix.

  Enter: (−) 2 ENTER 1 ENTER (−) 4 ENTER

- Matrix B will represent the equation $2x + y = -4$. Press
  MATRX , highlight **EDIT**, and select **2:[B]**. Define the matrix as one
  row and three columns.

  Enter: 1 ENTER 3 ENTER

  Then enter the values in the matrix.

  Enter: 2 ENTER 1 ENTER (−) 4 ENTER

  Press 2nd MODE [QUIT] to return to the **Home Screen.**

- To eliminate the variable y, multiply matrix A by -1 and add matrix B.

  Enter: [(-)] **1** [MATRX] **1** (to select [A]) [+] [MATRX] **2** (to select [B]) [ENTER]

  Enter the equation $(4x + 0y = 0)$ from the answer matrix on the calculator.

  Enter: 4 [X,T,θ,n] [+] **0** [ALPHA] **1** [Y] [2nd] [MATH] [TEST] **1** (to select =) **0** [ENTER]

  Solve this equation and store the value of x.

  Enter: 0 [STO▸] [X,T,θ,n] [ENTER]

- To eliminate the variable x, add matrix A and matrix B.

  Enter: [MATRX] **1** (to select [A]) [+] [MATRX] **2** (to select [B]) [ENTER]

  Enter the equation $(0x + 2y = -8)$ from the answer matrix on the calculator.

  Enter: 0 [X,T,θ,n] [+] **2** [ALPHA] **1** [Y] [2nd] [MATH] [TEST] **1** (to select =) [(-)] **8** [ENTER]

  Solve this equation and store the value of y.

  Enter: [(-)] **4** [STO▸] [ALPHA] **1** [Y] [ENTER]

  The solution of the system of equations is $(0, -4)$.

- Check the solution by entering each equation into the calculator.

  Enter: [(-)] **2** [X,T,θ,n] [+] [ALPHA] **1** [Y] [2nd] [MATH] [TEST] **1** (to select =) [(-)] **4** [ENTER]

  The 1.000 indicates that $(0, -4)$ is a solution of the equation $-2x + y = -4$.

  Enter: [(-)] **2** [X,T,θ,n] [+] [ALPHA] **1** [Y] [2nd] [MATH] [TEST] **1** (to select =) [(-)] **4**

  The 1.000 indicates that $(0, -4)$ is a solution of the equation $2x + y = -4$. Since $(0, -4)$ is a solution to each equation, it is the solution to the system of equations.

Graphing Calculator Activity 6

Solving Systems of Linear Equations

Practice

Solve each system of equations.

1. $5x - y = 5$
$-4x + 5y = 17$

2. $x + 3y = 12$
$x - y = 8$

3. $2x + 3y = 1$
$-3x + y = 15$

4. $2x + 7y = 3$
$x = 1 - 4y$

5. $3x - 5y = 11$
$x - 3y = 1$

6. $4x = 3y + 3$
$x = y - 1$

Graphing Calculator Activity 7

TEACHING SUGGESTIONS

Exploring Quadratic Functions

Objective   The student will solve quadratic equations in one variable both algebraically and graphically. Graphing calculators will be used both as a primary tool in solving problems and to verify algebraic solutions.

Use with GLENCOE Algebra 1: Integration, Applications, and Connections		
Lesson	Lesson Title	Student Edition Pages
11-1	Graphing Quadratic Functions	611-617
11-2	Solving Quadratic Equations by Graphing	620-627

Hints

- Each calculator has particular protocols with certain procedures. You may find it helpful to practice each lesson before teaching it.

For the CASIO CFX-9850Ga PLUS

The following explanation is designed to give an overview of the methods and options available when graphing and working with quadratic functions. For this example, screens for the function $y = x^2 + 5x + 6$ are used.

Graph Menu

- Before you begin graphing, check the calculator setup. From the **MAIN MENU**, select **5** **[GRAPH]**. Then press   SHIFT   MENU   **[SET UP]** and match the settings shown below.

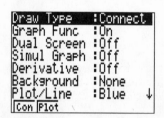 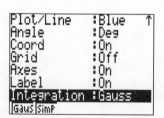

- Clear any existing equations by highlighting the equation and pressing   F2   **[DEL]** and   F1   **[YES]**.

- The equation to be graphed is entered in the same way that a linear equation is entered. Students use the x^2 to enter the exponent. For example, to enter $y = x^2 + 5x + 6$, press   X,θ,T x^2 +   5   X,θ,T   +   6.

- To view the graph, press   F6   **[DRAW]**.

NOTE: There are several choices for defining the view window.

- SHIFT   F3   allows the choice of   F3   **[STD]** (the standard viewing window) or   F1   **[INIT]** (the square viewing window).

- Selecting   F2   **[ZOOM]**   F6   [▷]   F4   **[INTG]** while the graph is drawn, redraws the graph so that the domain (*x*-values) changes by intervals of one unit.

- Select   F2   **[ZOOM]**   F6   [▷]   F4   **[INTG]**   F1   **[Trace]** and use the right and left arrow keys to explore the graph using integer values for *x*.

Graphing Calculator Activity 7 (continued)
TEACHING SUGGESTIONS

Activity 7

- When the graph is displayed, press F5 [G-Solv] to find special values from the graph.

  F1 [ROOT] finds the x-intercept.

  F2 [MAX] and F3 [MIN] find the maximum or minimum points of the function.

  F4 [Y-ICPT] finds the y-intercept.

  F6 [▷] and then F1 [Y-CAL] finds the y value for a specific x value. Likewise, if F2 [X-CAL] is selected, the x value for a specific y value can be found. Once an option is selected, the calculator will prompt you for the specific value to be entered. After entering the value, press EXE and wait. It will take the calculator a few seconds to calculate the value. In either case, the point is highlighted and its coordinates will be displayed on the screen. The screen at the right shows the x and y values for the equation $y = x^2 + 5x + 6$.

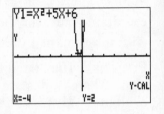

Conics Menu

- From the **MAIN MENU** select **9 [CONICS]**.

- In the **Select Equation** window use the down arrow to highlight the equation **Y = Ax² + Bx + C**, and press EXE.

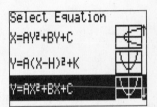

- Define the quadratic function by entering the value for A, pressing EXE, entering the value for B, pressing EXE, entering the value for C, and pressing EXE. By pressing F6 [DRAW], the graph will be displayed.

- With the graph displayed press F5 [G-SOLV]. The calculator will find and show the axis of symmetry by selecting F2 [SYM] and the vertex by selecting F4 [VTX].

Creating A Table Of Values

- At the **MAIN MENU**, select **7 [TABLE]**. If you have already entered an equation in the **GRAPH MENU** it will also appear in the **TABLE MENU**.

- Highlight any unwanted equations and delete by pressing F2 [DEL] F1 [YES]. Enter your equation if it has not already been entered.

- Press EXIT to return to the **Table Func:Y=** screen.

- Once the equation is entered, press SHIFT MENU [SET UP] and match those shown below. The first screen is the first half of the menu and the second screen is the last half of the menu.

> **NOTE:** There are three types of equations you can define. Press F3 and select **Y=**, **r=**, or **Parm.**

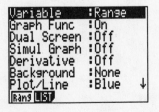
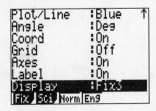

Graphing Calculator Activity 7 (continued)
TEACHING SUGGESTIONS

NOTE: Under **Display** if you see **FIX3/E** press F4 [Eng] to change from engineering mode to fixed decimal mode.

- Press EXIT to return to the **TABLE FUNC :Y=** screen. To define the desired x-interval (domain) for a table of coordinate pairs, press F5 [RANG]. For example, to show coordinate pairs for the function $y = x^2 + 5x + 6$ starting at $x = -6$ and ending in $x = 2$ with intervals of 1 unit, press (−) **6** EXE **2** EXE **1** EXE EXIT.

  Press F6 [TABL] and the table of values will appear as shown at the right. The y values are labeled by the number of the equation being evaluated (**Y1, Y2,** and so on).

  To select or deselect a function use F1 [SEL] in the **TABLE FUNC** screen. When selected, the function will have a dark square over the = sign.

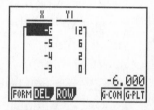

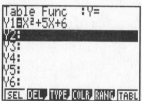

- With the table displayed, press F5 [G-CON] to see a line graph of the function or press F6 [G-PLT] to see a scatterplot of the table values. Press EXIT or F6 [G↔T] to return to the table.

NOTE: Pressing F6 [G↔T] repeatedly toggles the screen back and forth between the scatterplot and the table. The calculator will use the defined range and create a table of values for up to twenty functions and display them all. To see values for a function not in the current window, use the right or left arrow keys to move to the desired column.

For the TI-83

The following explanation is designed to give an overview of the methods and options available when graphing and working with quadratic functions. For this example, screens for the function $y = x^2 + 5x + 6$ are used.

Graphing a Quadratic Equation

- Before you begin graphing, check the calculator setup. From the **Home Screen**, press MODE and be sure all settings match those shown in the first screen below. Then press 2nd ZOOM [FORMAT] and be sure the settings match those in the second screen.

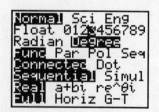

- Press Y= . Clear any existing equations by highlighting them and pressing CLEAR . Use the up or down arrows to move from one equation to another. Turn off the statistical graphs by pressing 2nd Y= [STAT PLOT], selecting 4:PlotsOff, and pressing ENTER . Set the viewing window to the standard viewing window by pressing ZOOM and selecting 6:Zstandard. Pressing 2nd MODE [QUIT] will return you to the **Home Screen**.

- The equation to be graphed is entered in the same way that a linear equation is entered. Students use the x^2 to enter the exponent. For example, to enter $y = x^2 + 5x + 6$, press Y= and enter the equation into **Y1=**: X,T,θ,n x^2 + 5 X,T,θ,n + 6 ENTER .

- To view the graph, press GRAPH .

- After the graph is displayed, you can choose a value for x and have the y value calculated. Suppose $y = x^2 + 5x + 6$ is graphed. Press 2nd TRACE [CALC] and select **1:value** and enter the desired x value, such as -2. (See first screen at the right.) Press ENTER . The equation, the x value, the y value, and the points are displayed on the graph. The second screen shows the result when -2 is entered for x. Press GRAPH or CLEAR to display the original graph.

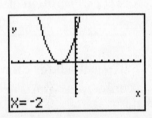

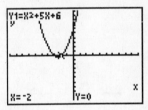

- To see the zeros of this function, it is helpful to zoom in on the area where the zeros occur. Press ZOOM , select **8:Zinterger**, and press ENTER . To zoom in on the area move the cursor toward the area where the zero seems to occur and press ZOOM , select **2:Zoom In**, and press ENTER . Zoom in again with the same keystrokes: ZOOM , **2:Zoom In**, and ENTER .

NOTE: There are several choices for defining the viewing window from the **ZOOM** menu. Pressing ZOOM 4 or ZOOM 5 or ZOOM 8 ENTER give the decimal, square, and integer windows, respectively. These windows are recommended for student exploration of the graphed functions. Pressing WINDOW allows students to set each value in the view-window manually.

- Select **4:ZDecimal** and the graph is redrawn. Press TRACE and use the right and left arrow keys. The change in the x values is $\frac{1}{10}$ of a unit.

- Selecting **5:ZSquare** redraws the graph with a square window. Press TRACE and use the right and left arrow keys. The change in the x values is $\frac{1}{10}$ of a unit.

- Selecting **6:ZStandard** redraws the graph with the standard window. Press TRACE and use the right and left arrow keys. The change in the x values is approximately 0.213 unit.

- Select **8:ZInteger** and the previous graph is displayed. Use the right and left arrow keys to move the cursor to the center of what will be the new screen. (The x- and y-axes will no longer be the center of the screen.) When the center is determined, press ENTER . The graph is redrawn. Press TRACE and use the right and left arrow keys. The domain (x values) now change by intervals of one unit.

- With the graph displayed pressing [2nd] [TRACE] **[CALC]** and selecting **2:zero** allows the student to find the zero (*x*-intercept) of a function. Students should understand that a zero occurs where the graph crosses the *x*-axis so that they can define the interval in which they will look for the exact value of the zero.

- In determining the zero of a function, the calculator looks for a **Left Bound** and **Right Bound** to determine the interval in which the zero occurs. When prompted to define the **Left Bound**, use the left arrow key to move the cursor to any point left of the point where the graph crosses the *x*-axis and press [ENTER].

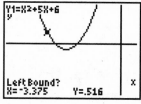

  The calculator now prompts you to define a **Right Bound**. Use the right arrow key to move the cursor to the left of the zero and press [ENTER].

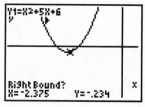

NOTE: Caution students not to move too far to the right or they miss a zero value if there is more than one.

The calculator then prompts you to enter a guess for the zero. You may enter your guess or press [ENTER] and the actual zero coordinates will appear.

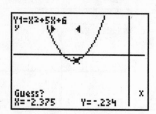
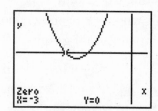

To find the other root use the same procedure as above.

- Press [2nd] [TRACE] and select **3:minimum** or **4:maximum** and use the same procedure of defining bounds to find a minimum or maximum value of the function in a given interval.

Create a Table of Values

- To create a table of values from the **Home Screen**, press [2nd] [WINDOW] **[TBLSET]**. The cursor will blink at **TblStart =**. Enter a starting *x* value. To start the values at −6, press [(−)] **6** [ENTER] and set the increment for the *x* values as 1 by making sure Δ**Tbl = 1**.

- Press [2nd] [GRAPH] **[TABLE]** and a table of values appears for the function **Y1 = x² + 5x + 6** beginning with −6.

NOTE: Using the up and down arrows scrolls the calculator screen to find as many values as necessary. The calculator will store 10 functions (**Y1, Y2, Y3**, and so on) and display 10 tables of values based on the defined *x* value starting point. Use the right and left arrow keys to move from one function to another.

- To select or deselect a function to appear as a table, press [Y=] and move the blinking cursor over the equals sign. Press [ENTER]. If the = sign is covered by a dark square that function is selected. If the = sign has no dark square, that function has been deselected. When deselected a table of values will not be generated by the calculator.

Answers for Student Worksheet Practice

Answers will vary depending on students' selections of x values. The coordinates of the vertex, the approximate roots, and sample graphs are given. Depending on the viewing screen selected, the approximate roots and screens may vary.

Vertex	Roots	CASIO CFX-9850Ga PLUS	TI-83
1. $(-4, -11)$	$x = -0.68,$ $x = -7.32$	Y1=X²+8X+5 X=-4 Y=-11 MIN	Y1=X²+8X+5 X=-4 Y=-11
2. $(-3, 0)$	$x = -3$	Y1=X²+6X+9 X=-3 Y=0 MIN	Y1=X²+6X+9 X=-3 Y=0
3. $(1, 1)$	no real roots	Y1=X²-2X+2 X=1 Y=1 MIN	Y1=X²-2X+2 X=1 Y=1
4. $(5, -4)$	$x = 3,$ $x = 7$	Y1=X²-10X+21 X=5 Y=-4 MIN	Y1=X²-10X+21 X=5 Y=-4
5. $(3.5, -6.25)$	$x = 1,$ $x = 6$	Y1=X²-7X+6 X=3.5 Y=-6.25 MIN	Minimum X=3.5 Y=-6.25

Algebra 1 Graphing Calculator Activities

Graphing Calculator Activity 7

Exploring Quadratic Functions

You can use the graphing calculator to graph quadratic functions and to find the zeros of the function. Recall that a quadratic equation is the quadratic function where $f(x) = 0$. The solutions of a quadratic equation are called roots. The roots of a quadratic equation can be found by finding the zeros of the quadratic function. Zeros are the values of x where the graph of the function touches or crosses the x-axis.

Graph the quadratic function $f(x) = x^2 + 5x + 6$ using paper and pencil. Verify your graph using the graphing calculator.

- The general form of a quadratic function is $f(x) = ax^2 + by + c$. For the function $f(x) = x^2 + 5x + 6$; $a = 1$, $b = 5$, and $c = 6$.

- Make a table of values. Start with the vertex of the function. Use the equation $x = -\frac{b}{2a}$ to find the axis of symmetry and the x-coordinate of the vertex. Evaluate $f\left(-\frac{b}{2a}\right)$ to find the y-coordinate of the vertex.

- Select other points on either side of the axis of symmetry. Remember that a quadratic function is symmetric.

- You can use the graphing calculator to determine points on the graph of $f(x) = x^2 + 5x + 6$. First, store the values for a and b in the calculator. Start at the **MAIN MENU**.

  Enter: 1 [RUN] 1 → ALPHA X,θ,T [A] EXE 5 → ALPHA log [B] EXE

- Then find the axis of symmetry and store this value of x.

  Enter: (−) ALPHA log [B] ab/c 2 ALPHA X,θ,T [A] EXE F↔D SHIFT (−) [Ans] → X,θ,T EXE

  You have found that the axis of symmetry $\left(x = -\frac{b}{2a}\right)$ is $x = -2.5$. The x-coordinate of the vertex is -2.5.

- To find the y-coordinate of the vertex, evaluate the quadratic function for $f(-2.5)$.

  Enter: X,θ,T | x^2 | + | 5 | X,θ,T | + | 6 | EXE | F↔D

  The y-coordinate of the vertex is -0.25. Therefore, the vertex is $(-2.5, -0.25)$.

- To make a table of values, press MENU 7 [TABLE]. If other equations are present, delete them by highlighting them and pressing F2 [DEL] F1 [YES]. Enter the equation.

  Enter: X,θ,T | x^2 | + | 5 | X,θ,T | + | 6 | EXE

  Press F5 [RANG]. Choose the start and end x values to be the same distance from the x-coordinate of the vertex (-2.5). For this function, add 4 to -2.5 and add -4 to -2.5.

  Enter: (-) 6.5 EXE 1.5 EXE 1 EXE EXIT F6 [TABL]

  A table with x and y values will appear.

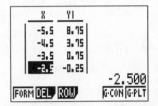

- To begin graphing the points, use the arrow keys to scroll down to the coordinates of the vertex. Sketch the graph on paper using the points listed in the graphing calculator table. To check if your points show a good quadratic function, press F6 [G-PLT]. If you don't see the familiar U-shaped curve, use the arrow keys to adjust the range values accordingly.

- Verify your sketch using the graphing calculator. From the **MAIN MENU**, press 5 [GRAPH]. The quadratic function $f(x) = x^2 + 5x + 6$ is already entered. Press SHIFT F3 [V-WIN] F3 [STD] EXIT F6 [DRAW]. Compare your graph to the graph on your calculator.

Estimate the roots (zeros) of the function using the graph you drew. Use the graphing calculator to verify the roots.

- To estimate the roots on the hand-drawn graph, find where the graph crosses the x-axis. The points should be somewhere near $(-3, 0)$ and $(-2, 0)$.

- To estimate the roots on the graphing calculator, with the graph drawn press SHIFT F1 [TRCE]. In **Trace Mode**, the cursor starts at the extreme left x value (-10 in the standard window). Use the right arrow key to find where the graph crosses the x-axis. The first root seems to be between $x = -3.016$ and $x = -2.857$.

- Check for an integer value.

  Enter: [SHIFT] [F2] [ZOOM] [F6] [▷] [F4] [INTG] [SHIFT] [F1] [TRACE]

  Hold down the right arrow key until the cursor appears. Then continue to move the cursor right until $x = -3$ and $y = 0$ appears. Pressing the right arrow key again shows that $x = -2$ and $y = 0$. The roots of the quadratic equation are $x = -2$ and $x = -3$.

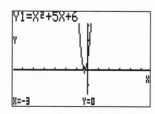 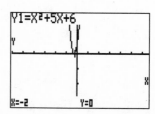

- You can use an alternate method to verify the roots. With the graph drawn, press [SHIFT] [F5] [G-SLV]. Then press [F1] [ROOT]. After a few seconds, the calculator finds and displays the left-most root. Press the right arrow key and the second root is displayed.

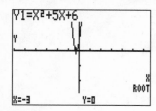 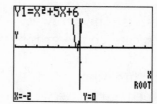

Graphing Calculator Activity 7

Exploring Quadratic Functions

You can use the graphing calculator to graph quadratic functions and to find the zeros of the function. Recall that a quadratic equation is the quadratic function where $f(x) = 0$. The solutions of a quadratic equation are called roots. The roots of a quadratic equation can be found by finding the zeros of the quadratic function. Zeros are the values of x where the graph of the function touches or crosses the x-axis.

Graph the quadratic function $f(x) = x^2 + 5x + 6$ using paper and pencil. Verify your graph using the graphing calculator.

- The general form of a quadratic function is $f(x) = ax^2 + by + c$. For the function $f(x) = x^2 + 5x + 6$; $a = 1$, $b = 5$, and $c = 6$.

- Make a table of values. Start with the vertex of the function. Use the equation $x = -\frac{b}{2a}$ to find the axis of symmetry and the x-coordinate of the vertex. Evaluate $f\left(-\frac{b}{2a}\right)$ to find the y-coordinate of the vertex.

- Select other points on either side of the axis of symmetry. Remember that a quadratic function is symmetric.

- You can use the graphing calculator to determine points on the graph of $f(x) = x^2 + 5x + 6$. First, store the values for a and b in the calculator. Start at the **Home Screen**.

  Enter: 1 STO▶ ALPHA MATH [A] ENTER **5** STO▶ ALPHA MATRX
  [B] ENTER

- Then find the axis of symmetry and store this value of x.

  Enter: (−) ALPHA MATRX [B] ÷ **2** ALPHA MATH [A] ENTER 2nd
  (−) [ANS] STO▶ X,T,θ,n ENTER

  You have found that the axis of symmetry $\left(x = -\frac{b}{2a}\right)$ is $x = -2.5$. The x-coordinate of the vertex is -2.5.

- To find the y-coordinate of the vertex, evaluate the quadratic function for $f(-2.5)$.

  Enter: X,T,θ,n x² + 5 X,T,θ,n + 6 ENTER

  The y-coordinate of the vertex is -0.25. Therefore the vertex is $(-2.5, -0.25)$.

- To make a table of values, press Y= . If other equations are present, delete them by pressing CLEAR . Enter the equation.

  Enter: X,T,θ,n x² + 5 X,T,θ,n + 6 ENTER

  Press 2nd WINDOW **[TBLSET]**. Choose the **Tblstart** value to be at least 4 units to the left of the x coordinate of the vertex (-2.5). For this function, add -4 to -2.5.

  Enter: (−) 6.5 ENTER .5 ENTER 2nd GRAPH **[TABLE]**

  A table with x and y values will appear.

- To begin graphing the points, use the arrow keys to scroll down to the coordinates of the vertex. Sketch the graph on paper using the points listed in the graphing calculator table.

X	Y₁	
-5.500	8.750	
-5.000	6.000	
-4.500	3.750	
-4.000	2.000	
-3.500	.750	
-3.000	0.000	
-2.500	-.250	
X=-2.5		

- Verify your sketch using the graphing calculator. From the table of values press Y= . The quadratic function $f(x) = x^2 + 5x + 6$ is already entered. Press ZOOM and select **6:ZStandard**. Compare your graph to the graph on your calculator.

Estimate the zeros of the function using the graph you drew. Use the graphing calculator to verify the zeros.

- To estimate the zeros on the hand-drawn graph, find where the graph crosses the x-axis. The points should be somewhere near $(-3, 0)$ and $(-2, 0)$.

- To estimate the zeros on the graphing calculator, press TRACE . In **Trace Mode**, the cursor starts at the x- or y-intercept if possible. Use the arrow keys to find where the graph crosses the x-axis. The zero on the right seems to be between $x = -1.915$ and $x = -2.128$.

- To check for an integer value, place the cursor near the first zero.

  Enter: [ZOOM] **8** (to select **ZInteger**) [ENTER] [ZOOM] **2** (to select
  Zoom In) [ENTER] [ZOOM] **2** (to select **Zoom In**) [ENTER]

  This procedure magnifies the graph and makes it easier to locate
  the zeros visually. Press [TRACE] and move the cursor to $x = -2$
  and $y = 0$. Continue to move the cursor left to find the second zero
  at $x = -3$ and $y = 0$. The zeros of the quadratic equation are
  $x = -2$ and $x = -3$.

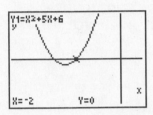
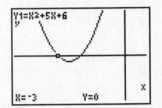

- You can use an alternate method to verify the zeros. With the
  graph drawn, press [2nd] [TRACE] **[CALC]** and select **2:Zero**. The
  calculator will ask for an x value to the left of the zero you are
  determining. Move the cursor to the left of the zero and press
  [ENTER]. The calculator then asks for an x value to the right of the
  zero you are determining. Move the cursor to the right of the zero
  and press [ENTER]. The calculator now asks you to make a guess.
  Press [ENTER] and the zero value appears. Repeat this procedure
  beginning with [2nd] [TRACE] **[CALC]** to find the second zero.

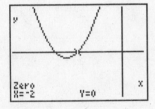
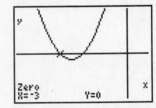

Exploring Quadratic Functions

Practice

For each quadratic function, complete the following.

A. *Construct a table of seven values using the vertex of the function as the middle value.*

B. *Using the graphing calculator, graph the function. Estimate the roots of the quadratic equation. If integral roots cannot be found, state the consecutive integers between which the roots lie. If no roots can be found, write NO REAL ROOTS.*

C. *Use the graphing calculator to verify the roots.*

1. $f(x) = x^2 + 8x + 5$

Vertex

x							
y							

Roots are _____. Sketch the graph.

2. $f(x) = x^2 + 6x + 9$

Vertex

x							
y							

Roots are _____. Sketch the graph.

3. $f(x) = x^2 - 2x + 2$

Vertex

x							
y							

Roots are _____. Sketch the graph.

4. $f(x) = x^2 - 10x + 21$

Vertex

x							
y							

Roots are _____. Sketch the graph.

5. $f(x) = x^2 - 7x + 6$

Vertex

x							
y							

Roots are _____. Sketch the graph.

M^3—Mean, Median, and Mode

Objective   The student will compare multiple one-variable data sets; using statistical techniques that include measure of central tendency, range, stem-and-leaf plots, and box-and-whisker plots.

Use with GLENCOE Algebra 1: Integration, Applications, and Connections		
Lesson	**Lesson Title**	**Student Edition Pages**
3-7	**Integration: Statistics** Measures of Central Tendency	178-183
7-7	**Integration: Statistics** Box-and-Whisker Plots	427-434

Hints

- Each calculator has particular protocols with certain procedures. You may find it helpful to practice each lesson before teaching it.

- This activity is based on data acquired from students.

- **Materials Needed:** metric measuring tape, masking tape, poster board, and marking pens

For the CASIO CFX-9850Ga PLUS

To enter data:
- From the **MAIN MENU**, press **2 [STAT]** F6 [▷]. Delete all unwanted lists by highlighting each list name and pressing F4 **[DEL-A]** F1 **[YES]**.

- Enter data by pressing the appropriate number keys followed by EXE .

To edit data:
- To delete a specific entry, highlight it and press F3 **[DEL]**.

- To insert data highlight where you want it to be and press F5 **[INS]**. Then type in the new value. (Be sure to press EXE after each new value.)

To order data:
- Highlight the list to be ordered and choose F1 **[SRT-A]** to sort in ascending order (from smallest to largest) or F2 **[SRT-D]** to sort in descending order (from largest to smallest).

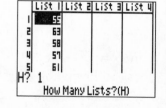

- The calculator will ask **How Many Lists?(H)** and you will type in the number of lists that you want sorted. Then press EXE .

- The calculator will then ask for the base list if there are more than one. Choose the base list by typing in its number and EXE . You will be asked to enter the number of each additional list to be included in the sort. Do so and press EXE after each choice.

NOTE: When in the **STAT Mode** you may have to press F6 [▷] to access the above choices.

To graph your data:
- In **STAT Mode** press F1 **[GRPH]**. If **GRPH** is not at the bottom left of the screen, press F6 [▷] and repeat the above entry.

Graphing Calculator Activity 8 (continued)
TEACHING SUGGESTIONS

- Press [F6] [SET] and highlight the following for each category. The screen should look like the one at the right.

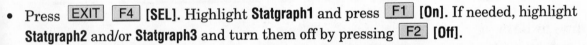

Statgraph	Press [F1] [GPH1]
Graph Type	Press [F6] [▷] [F2] [Box]
Xlist	Press [F1] [List1]
Frequency	Press [F1] [1]
Graph Color	(student's choice)
Outliers	Press [F1] [On]

- Press [EXIT] [F4] [SEL]. Highlight **Statgraph1** and press [F1] [On]. If needed, highlight **Statgraph2** and/or **Statgraph3** and turn them off by pressing [F2] [Off].

- To draw the box-plot (box-and-whisker plot), press [F6] [DRAW].

To find the mean, median, mode, and other statistics:
- Press [F1] [1VAR].

NOTE: If the data is multi-modal the calculator chooses the largest modal value to display. If there is no mode the largest data value is displayed.

FOR THE TI-83

To clear a list:
- To clear *all* existing lists, press [2nd] [+] [MEM], select **4:ClrAllLists**, and press [ENTER].

- There are two ways to clear individual lists:

  Press [STAT], select **4:ClrList**, and enter the list to be cleared by pressing [2nd] followed by the number associated with the list, *OR*

  Press [STAT], select **1:Edit**, highlight the list name by using the arrow keys, and press [CLEAR] [ENTER].

To enter data:
- Press [2nd] [STAT] and select **1:Edit**. Enter data by pressing the appropriate number keys followed by [ENTER].

To edit data:
- To delete a specific entry, highlight it and press [DEL]. To insert data, highlight where you want it to be inserted and press [2nd] [DEL] [INS]. Type in the new value and press [ENTER].

Activity 8

To order data:

- Press [STAT] and select **2:SortA(**. Then enter the name of the list to be sorted by pressing [2nd] and the number of the list. This sorts the list in ascending order (from smallest to largest). To sort a list in descending order, press [STAT] and select **3:SortD(**. Then enter the list to be sorted as described above.

NOTE: To sort more than one list, enter the list names separated by a comma. For example, to sort lists 1 and 2 in descending order, use **SortD(L1,L2)**. Each list will be sorted separately. Lists will not be linked or combined.

To graph your data:

- Press [2nd] [Y=] **[STATPLOT]** and select **1:Plot1**. Then make the following selections so that the screen matches the one shown at the right. Be sure to press [ENTER] after each selection.

On Off	Highlight **On** and press [ENTER].
Type:	Select the first (modified) box plot. Press [ENTER].
XList:	Enter list 1 by pressing [2nd] **1 [L1]** [ENTER].
Freq:	Enter **1.**
Mark	(student's choice)

- Press [GRAPH].

NOTE: A modified box plot displays the outliers. The whisker will not contain the outlier unless the outlier is the maximum or minimum point.

To find the mean, median, and other statistics:

- Press [STAT], highlight **CALC**, and select **1:1-Var Stats** [ENTER].

NOTE: The mode is not displayed on this calculator.

Answers for Student Worksheet Practice

1. Sample graph:

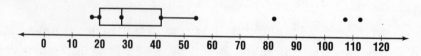

2. **a.** 50%   **b.** 25%   **c.** 75%   **d.** 50%   **e.** 25%

3. Yes; Sample answer: One quartile has a greater range than the other.

4. Sample answer: Because it is the middle value of the data.

5. mean = 40; number of data = 16; minimum x value = 18; median = 28; maximum x value = 112; mode = 18, 19, 22, 29

6. Sample answer: The mean is the arithmetic average of all of the values, while the median is the value for which half the data lies below the value and half lies above the data.

Graphing Calculator Activity 8

M³—Mean, Median, and Mode

You can use the graphing calculator to make a box-and-whisker plot and to find measures of central tendency.

Make a list of the heights of your classmates. Use the graphing calculator to make a box-and-whisker plot and to find measures of central tendency for the data.

- With a partner, define each term.

  mean _____

  _____

  median _____

  _____

  mode _____

  _____

  Compare your definitions with another pair of students.

- Measure the height of your partner. You may want to place a piece of tape on the wall to mark the height of your partner. Then use a tape measure to determine the distance from the bottom of the piece of tape to the floor. Record your partner's height on the class data chart.

- You are now ready to enter the data into your calculator. From the **MAIN MENU**, press **2 [STAT]**. Highlight **List 1** and press F6 [▷] F4 **[DEL-A]** F1 **[YES]**. Enter the data from the class chart by pressing each number followed by EXE.

- Sort the data in ascending order. If **SRT-A** does not appear in the lower left side of the window, press F6 [▷]. Then press F1 **[SRT-A]**.

- The calculator asks **How Many Lists?(H)**. At the blinking cursor enter **1** EXE. The calculator now asks **Select List(L)**. At the blinking cursor enter **1** EXE. You will see the data listed from smallest data point to largest.

- Use the graphing calculator to make a box-and-whisker plot. First press F6 [▷] F1 [GRPH] F6 [SET] and highlight the following for each category.

  Highlight **StatGraph1** and press F1 [GPH1].

  Highlight **Graph Type** and press F6 [▷] F2 [Box].

  Highlight **Xlist** and press F1 [List1].

  Highlight **Frequency** and press F1 [1].

  Highlight **Graph Color** and enter your choice of color by pressing F1 , F2 , or F3 .

  Finally, highlight **Outliers** and press F1 [On].

  The screen should look like the one at the right.

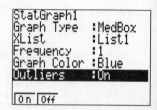

Enter: EXIT F4 [SEL]

Highlight **StatGraph1** and press F1 [On]. Be sure **StatGraph2** and **StatGraph3** read **DrawOff**. Press F6 [DRAW] to draw the graph.

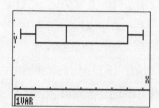

- Use the graphing calculator to find measures of central tendency.

  Enter: F1 [1VAR]

  The statistical values are displayed. Use the down arrow key to view all of the information.

NOTE: If the data is multi-modal the calculator chooses the largest modal value to display. If there is no mode, the largest data value is displayed. (This is a false mode.)

- To go back to the graph, press F6 [DRAW]. From the graph, press SHIFT F1 [TRCE]. Use the right arrow key and locate the minimum data value (**MinX**), the first quartile value (**Q1**), the median (**Med**), the third quartile value (**Q3**), and the maximum data value (**MaxX**).

Graphing Calculator Activity 8 (continued)

- Return to the screen displaying the statistics.

  Enter: F1 F1 [1-VAR]

  Fill in the following information.

  $\bar{x}$ = _____

  n = _____

  minX = _____

  Med = _____

  maxX = _____

  Mod* = _____

  *Check your data to see if it is multi-modal or if there is no mode.

Summary

Describe, in complete sentences, what you discovered about this
set of data. Include each statistical component listed above in your
summary.

_____

_____

_____

M³—Mean, Median, and Mode

You can use the graphing calculator to make a box-and-whisker plot and to find measures of central tendency.

Make a list of the heights of your classmates. Use the graphing calculator to make a box-and-whisker plot and to find measures of central tendency for the data.

- With a partner, define each term.

  mean _____

  _____

  median _____

  _____

  mode _____

  _____

  Compare your definitions with another pair of students.

- Measure the height of your partner. You may want to place a piece of tape on the wall to mark the height of your partner. Then use a tape measure to determine the distance from the bottom of the piece of tape to the floor. Record your partner's height on the class data chart.

- You are now ready to enter the data into your calculator. From the **Home Screen**, press STAT and select **1:Edit**. Highlight **L1** and press CLEAR ENTER. Enter the data from the class chart by pressing each number followed by ENTER.

- Sort the data in ascending order.

  Enter: STAT 2 (to select **SortA**) 2nd 1 [L1] ENTER

  Done appears on the screen. To go back to the list screen, press STAT and select **1:Edit**. You will see the data listed in ascending order.

- Use the graphing calculator to make a box-and-whisker plot. First press Y= and make sure all graphs are either cleared or deselected.

Enter: 2nd Y= [STAT PLOT] **1** (to select **Plot1...Off**)

Highlight **On** and press ENTER. Then choose the type of graph.

Enter: ▼ ▶ ▶ ▶ ENTER

Choose the **Xlist**.

Enter: ▼ 2nd **1** [L1] ENTER

Determine the frequency.

Enter: ALPHA **1** ENTER

Finally, choose a type of mark, highlight it, and press ENTER. Your screen should be similar to the one at the right.

Enter: ZOOM **9** (to select **ZoomStat**) GRAPH

The graph is drawn.

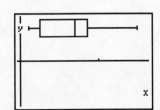

NOTE: **ZoomStat** redefines the viewing window to include all data points.

- Use the graphing calculator to find measures of central tendency.

Enter: STAT ▶ (to highlight **CALC**) **1** (to select **Var Stats**) 2nd
    1 [L1] ENTER

The statistical values are displayed. Use the down arrow key to view all of the information.

NOTE: The TI-83 does not display the mode. It must be found by inspecting the data.

- To go back to the graph, press GRAPH . From the graph, press TRACE . Use the right/left arrow keys and locate the minimum data value (**minX**), the first quartile value (**QI**), the median (**Med**), the third quartile value (**Q3**), and the maximum data value (**maxX**).

NOTE: The plot number graphed and the list containing the data points are displayed in the upper left corner.

- Return to the screen displaying the statistics.

    Enter: STAT ▶ (to highlight **CALC**) **1** (to select **Var Stats**) 2nd
    1 [L1] ENTER

    Fill in the following information.

    $\bar{x}$ = _____

    n = _____

    MinX = _____

    Med = _____

    MaxX = _____

    Mod* = _____

    *Check your data to see if it is multi-modal or if there is no mode.

Summary

Describe, in complete sentences, what you discovered about this set of data. Include each statistical component listed above in your summary.

_____

_____

_____

NAME ______________________ DATE ______________

Graphing Calculator Activity 8

Student Worksheet

M³—Mean, Median, and Mode

Practice

1992 Summer Olympics Top 16 Medal Winners	
Team	***Total Number of Medals Won***
Unified Team	112
U.S.A.	108
Germany	82
China	54
Cuba	31
Hungary	30
South Korea	29
France	29
Australia	27
Spain	22
Japan	22
Britain	20
Italy	19
Poland	19
Canada	18
Romania	18

Source: *The World Almanac,* 1995

Use the information in the table to complete each of the following.

1. Using the graphing calculator, make a box-and-whisker plot of the data. Sketch your graph below.

2. About what percent of the teams are represented by each section of the box-and-whisker plot?

a. below the median ______________

b. below the lower quartile ______________

c. above the lower quartile ______________

d. in the box ______________

e. on each whisker ______________

3. Is one whisker longer than the other? What do you think this means?

_____

_____

_____

4. Why isn't the median in the center of the box?

_____

_____

_____

5. Find each value.

mean = _____

number of data = _____

minimum x value = _____

median = _____

maximum x value = _____

mode* = _____

*Check your data to see if it is multi-modal or if there is no mode.

6. In complete sentences, explain the difference between the mean and the median of the data.

_____

_____

_____